CD 1

 P9-DCC-302

 **CD 2**

TRACK *1*   *I Love Lucy:* "Lucy Does a TV Commercial–
       Vitameatavegamin"

TRACK *2*   *The Ed Sullivan Show:* **Elvis Debuts**

TRACK *3*   *The Dick Van Dyke Show:* **"That's My Boy?"**

TRACK *4*   *The Fugitive:* **"The Judgment"**

TRACK *5*   *All in the Family:* **"Sammy's Visit"**

TRACK *6*   *The Brady Bunch:* **"The Subject Was Noses"**

TRACK *7*   *Saturday Night Live:* **The Early Years**

TRACK *8*   *Dallas:* **"Who Done It?"**

TRACK *9*   *M*A*S*H:* **"Goodbye, Farewell, and Amen"**

TRACK *10*   *Cheers:* **"I'll Be Seeing You"**

TRACK *11*   *The Tonight Show Starring Johnny Carson:*
       "Funny Moments and a Final Farewell"

TRACK *12*   *Survivor:* **Season One**

TRACK *13*   **Nixon's Checkers Speech**

TRACK *14*   **The First Great Debate: Kennedy versus Nixon**

TRACK *15*   **Four Days in November**

TRACK *16*   **Vietnam: Cronkite Denounces the War**

TRACK *17*   **Television in Space**

TRACK *18*   **Nixon: From Watergate to Resignation**

TRACK *1*   **The TV Princess**

TRACK *2*   **The Rescue of Baby Jessica**

TRACK *3*   **The Fall of the Berlin Wall**

TRACK *4*   **Chasing O.J.**

TRACK *5*   **Presidential Election Night Coverage 2000**

TRACK *6*   **September 11th**

TRACK *7*   *Wide World of Sports*

TRACK *8*   **Home Run Kings: Maris, McGwire, Bonds**

TRACK *9*   **Black Power: The Protest at the 1968
       Mexico City Games**

TRACK *10*   **The *Heidi* Game**

TRACK *11*   *Monday Night Football*

TRACK *12*   **1972 Munich Olympics Crisis**

TRACK *13*   **The Battle of the Sexes**

TRACK *14*   **The Perfect 10s: Comaneci and Retton**

TRACK *15*   **Lake Placid 1980: "Do You Believe
       in Miracles?"**

TRACK *16*   **Ali Lights the Centennial Torch**

TRACK *17*   **Tiger's Win for the Ages**

DVD contents are arranged chronologically within the sections Entertainment, News, and Sports, in that order. Click on the appropriate category and then scroll down through the menu until the desired broadcast appears.

STAY TUNED

Television's Unforgettable Moments

Other Books by Joe Garner

We Interrupt This Broadcast
And the Crowd Goes Wild
And the Fans Roared
Echoes of Notre Dame Football

STAY TUNED

Television's Unforgettable Moments

Joe Garner

Andrews McMeel
Publishing

Kansas City

To all the talented people in front of and behind the camera
for a lifetime of unforgettable television moments—
and to Colleen, J.B., and Jillian for all the unforgettable moments of my lifetime.

Contents

Introduction ix

Unforgettable Moments in Television **Entertainment**

		PAGE	CD	TRACK
May 5, 1952	*I Love Lucy:* "Lucy Does a TV Commercial—*Vitameatavegamin*"	4	1	1
September 9, 1956	*The Ed Sullivan Show:* Elvis Debuts	8	1	2
September 25, 1963	*The Dick Van Dyke Show:* "That's My Boy?"	12	1	3
August 29, 1967	*The Fugitive:* "The Judgment"	16	1	4
February 19, 1972	*All in the Family:* "Sammy's Visit"	20	1	5
February 9, 1973	*The Brady Bunch:* "The Subject Was Noses"	24	1	6
1975 to 1980	*Saturday Night Live:* The Early Years	28	1	7
November 21, 1980	*Dallas:* "Who Done It?"	34	1	8
February 28, 1983	*M*A*S*H:* "Goodbye, Farewell, and Amen"	38	1	9

		PAGE	CD	TRACK
May 10, 1984	*Cheers:* "I'll Be Seeing You"	44	1	10
May 22, 1992	*The Tonight Show Starring Johnny Carson:* "Funny Moments and a Final Farewell"	48	1	11
August 24, 2000	*Survivor:* Season One	54	1	12

Unforgettable Moments in Television News

		PAGE	CD	TRACK
September 23, 1952	Nixon's Checkers Speech	60	1	13
September 26, 1960	The First Great Debate: Kennedy versus Nixon	64	1	14
November 22–25, 1963	Four Days in November	68	1	15
February 27, 1968	Vietnam: Cronkite Denounces the Vietnam War	74	1	16
February 20, 1962 *July 20, 1969* *January 28, 1986*	Television in Space	78	1	17
June 17, 1972, to *August 8, 1974*	Nixon: From Watergate to Resignation	84	1	18
July 29, 1981, to *September 6, 1997*	The TV Princess	90	2	1
October 14–16, 1987	The Rescue of Baby Jessica	96	2	2
November 9, 1989	The Fall of the Berlin Wall	100	2	3
June 17, 1994	Chasing O.J.	106	2	4
November 7, 2000	Presidential Election Night Coverage 2000	112	2	5
September 11, 2001	September 11th	118	2	6

Unforgettable Moments in Television **Sports**

		PAGE	CD	TRACK
April 29, 1961, to present	*Wide World of Sports*	126	2	7
October 1, 1961 *September 8, 1998* *October 5, 2001*	Home Run Kings: Maris, McGwire, Bonds	130	2	8
October 16, 1968	Black Power: The Protest at the 1968 Mexico City Games	136	2	9
November 17, 1968	The *Heidi* Game	140	2	10
September 21, 1970, *to present*	*Monday Night Football*	144	2	11
September 5, 1972	1972 Munich Olympics Crisis	148	2	12
September 20, 1973	The Battle of the Sexes	152	2	13
July 18, 1976, and *August 3, 1984*	The Perfect 10s: Comaneci and Retton	156	2	14
February 22, 1980	Lake Placid 1980: "Do You Believe in Miracles?"	160	2	15
July 19, 1996	Ali Lights the Centennial Torch	166	2	16
April 13, 1997	Tiger's Win for the Ages	172	2	17
	Acknowledgments	176		
	Credits	178		
	About the Author and Hosts	180		
	Photo Credits	182		

Introduction

I have always loved television.

As a child of the '60s growing up in the rural Midwest, TV was an integral part of my life. My earliest memories are of watching television with my holster buckled and my cowboy hat on, watching Roy Rogers tame the Wild West. And I'd have given anything if our dachshund could have done half the things Lassie could do. I couldn't begin to list all of my favorite shows over the years. And despite conventional wisdom that suggests that too much tube time dulls the creative senses, I believe it had just the opposite effect. It sparked my imagination, and some of my favorite shows like *Batman* and *Lost in Space* became the source for hours of pretend play. And even though I grew up in the pre-MTV, pre-24-hour cable news, pre-ESPN era, Dick Clark made sure I knew who and what was cool, Walter Cronkite summed up the world's events in a half hour every evening, and Jim McKay brought the whole wide world of sports into our living room on the weekend.

So it should come as no surprise that writing and producing *Stay Tuned: Television's Unforgettable Moments* was truly a thrill from start to finish. In the pages of the book and on the accompanying DVD and compact discs are the stories and excerpts of moments from television's half century that entertained, informed, inspired, disgusted, alienated, unified, concerned, horrified, comforted, and thrilled us. And at its best, television transformed us.

Over television's relatively brief existence, we have watched situation comedies evolve from *I Love Lucy* to *All in the Family* to *Will & Grace*, at first merely amusing and then becoming reflections of society pushing cultural boundaries. Television demonstrated its compatibility with politics—uniting the nation in the optimism of their first offspring, President John F. Kennedy, and dividing it through the exploits of President Richard Nixon. Television has taken us to scenes of celebration, such as the rescue of baby Jessica and the demolition of communism's wall in Berlin. Television provided a front-row seat to see Mary Lou become a perfect 10, Barry Bonds become the home run king, and Tiger walk in the paths of Jackie Robinson and Jack Nicklaus in pursuit of his "win for the ages!" We have watched as television exposed imperfections in society, in the jurors' box in the trial of O. J. Simpson, and the ballot box in election 2000. Television challenged us with game shows, first as contests of knowledge then of survival, with payoffs climbing from washer-dryers to cash of over a million bucks. Television has carried us around the globe, to the moon and beyond, and in the process helped us refine the vision of ourselves.

Stay Tuned: Television's Unforgettable Moments is a multimedia collection of these memorable images from entertainment, news, and sports television that captured our attention and left an indelible mark on the cultural, political, and social landscape. These are moments seared forever into our imaginations.

No other form of mass media can put us in the moment like television. Print can only describe it; radio allows us to eavesdrop on it. But television puts us in the middle of it. Don Hewitt, one of the architects of network television news and the executive producer of *60 Minutes*, described television as the nation's hearth, with the ability to entertain us, move us, and unify us. "Sometimes," he told me, "television is a theater. Sometimes it's a newsroom. Sometimes it's a movie house. Sometimes it's a sports stadium. And sometimes it's a chapel." The day of the Kennedy assassination, as on September 11th, all of America came to their television sets. "That is the best use of television," he said.

In most instances, I'll take you "behind the camera" through original interviews I conducted with the people responsible for creating these unforgettable moments—the writers, producers, and stars.

Along with Don Hewitt, many television luminaries sat for videotaped interviews that I have included on the DVD and compact discs. I was like a kid in a candy store talking with *I Love Lucy's* writing team of Bob Carroll Jr. and Madelyn Pugh-Davis about working with Lucy and how they came up with many of Lucy's classic moments, including Vitameatavegamin. *All in the Family* creator Norman Lear talked about the origins of TV's most famous kiss. *Meet the Press* host Tim Russert confessed his hair-pulling frustrations of covering election night 2000. I enjoyed listening to Frank Gifford speak candidly of what it was really like in the booth on Monday nights with Howard and "Dandy" Don. I was taken aback as *M*A*S*H* writer and executive producer Burt Metcalfe recalled the harrowing true stories of real M*A*S*H doctors who inspired much of what went into the series and its historic finale. And I was touched as Ed McMahon expressed the genuine admiration and affection he felt as he watched Johnny Carson say good night for the final time.

Selecting the moments to include in *Stay Tuned* was a difficult yet enormously enjoyable task. (Remember, it involved watching a lot of television.) In fact, I wish the project had been as simple as just choosing what I wanted to include. But without going into all of the gory details, I'm still trying to wash the stickiness of the endless red tape off my fingertips.

While I am certain that you could quickly list shows that you think should have been included, my criterion was not "unforgettable shows" but "unforgettable moments." Again, I have no doubt that you could create a lengthy list of "moments" that should have been included in this edition, but that's why sequels exist. The moments included in *Stay Tuned* are milestones in television's history because they were "firsts," because they achieved historic ratings, or for reasons hard to quantify even by those who created them.

As important as selecting the moments was choosing the guides to take you through television's past. I am thrilled to have such an esteemed trio whose careers span the existence of the medium itself. Television's most beloved performer, Dick Van Dyke, presents the unforgettable moments from entertainment television. Walter Cronkite, still television's most trusted and revered broadcast journalist, takes you through a half century of television news moments. (Little did I know that I was reuniting the original team of Cronkite and Van Dyke from CBS's *The Morning Show* circa 1954.) And Bob Costas, one of television's most accomplished broadcasters, hosts the exciting and memorable moments from television sports. It has been an honor and a pleasure to work with each of them.

What I hope you get from *Stay Tuned* are hours of enjoyment as you relive some of the funniest and most entertaining, informative, controversial, shocking, and moving moments in television's glorious history.

STAY TUNED

Unforgettable Moments in Television **Entertainment**

I Love Lucy

"Lucy Does a TV Commercial— *Vitameatavegamin*"

May 5, 1952

"Hello friends. . . . Are you tired, run down, and listless? Do you poop out at parties? Are you unpopular? The answer to all your problems is in this little bottle: Vitameatavegamin!"

Vitameatavegamin stirs up spoonfuls of memories of Lucille Ball and of her matchless comedic talent that made *I Love Lucy* one of America's most beloved television series and "Lucy Does a TV Commercial" one of the show's most memorable episodes.

Lucille Ball got her start in early 1940 as a contract player for MGM. She was cast in the film *Too Many Girls* along with a dashing young Cuban-born bandleader named Desi Arnaz. Ball admitted that she fell in love with Arnaz "wham, bang—in about five minutes." The two courted over the next several months, and on November 30, 1940, Lucille Ball and Desi Arnaz were married, destined to become one of the most powerful and famous couples in show business history.

While Ball continued her work in film, roles for Arnaz were scarce. Frustrated, he reassembled his band and began touring the country. But the insalubrious activities of the road took a toll on their marriage.

In July 1948, Ball agreed to star with actor Richard Denning in a new radio show for CBS. *My Favorite Husband*, adapted for radio from the book *Mr. and Mrs. Cugat* by

Left to right: Ball greets the studio audience before the show's live broadcast. ▪ Ethel and Fred with Lucy and Desi. ▪ Lucy tries to convince Desi to use her in his commercial.

Isobel Scott Rorick, centered on the travails of a scheming ditzy housewife and her long-suffering banker husband. The show became a hit and when CBS wanted *Husband* for television, Ball insisted Arnaz be her costar. The network, wary of a mixed marriage in prime time, claimed the couple wouldn't be believable. Undaunted, Ball and Arnaz created a live stage show; their national tour won rave reviews and convinced CBS.

At the time, television shows were shot live in New York. A low-quality 16 mm kinescope print was made by filming a TV screen during the live East Coast broadcast. That kinescope print was then shown to the rest of the country. Rather than shooting *I Love Lucy* the traditional way, Arnaz and Ball insisted on doing the show from Hollywood, since Ball was pregnant. Along with the show's cocreator Jess Oppenheimer, they came up with a unique proposal: *I Love Lucy* would be shot on 35 mm film, in front of a live audience, with three cameras. This innovation created a sharper image for audiences across the country, and ultimately television production shifted from New York to Hollywood.

Strangely, no one knows for certain who is responsible for the title change from *My Favorite Husband* to *I Love Lucy*, but in terms of star billing it was deftly diplomatic. As Ball pointed out, "People would know that the 'I' was Desi," and she was equally pleased that the word "Love" was included. *I Love Lucy* made its debut at 9 P.M. on Monday, October 15, 1951, and immediately became one of America's top-ranked shows for most of its six-year run. It was so popular, in fact, that telephone companies reported fewer calls while *Lucy* aired and Chicago's Marshall Field's department store moved its evening hours to Thursday. Their sign announced, "We love Lucy, too, so we're closing on Monday nights."

The first season was composed of 35 episodes. Episode number 30, titled "Lucy Does a TV Commercial," was filmed on March 28, 1952, and first aired on May 5, 1952. It has become one of the most memorable in television history.

In this episode Lucy learns that Ricky must hire a spokesmodel to do a commercial for a product called Vitameatavegamin that will air during his television special. Lucy pleads with Ricky to give her a chance to make the commercial but Ricky adamantly refuses, telling Lucy that he "needs someone with a lot of 'sperience.'" When the woman Ricky hired calls to speak to him, the irrepressible Lucy intercepts the call and tells her that she isn't needed after all, and then Lucy shows up at the studio in her place. At first she does fine, encouraging viewers to "spoon your way to health," although the tonic's awful taste produces

classic Lucy facial reactions. But then trouble arises: Besides vitamins, meat, vegetables, and minerals, Vitameatavegamin contains 23 percent alcohol.

Lucy tries desperately to sell both herself and the booze-laden health product, but repeated rehearsals leave her loopy and unable to spin her spiel without stumbling. After seven spoonfuls Lucy is so sloshed she can neither pronounce Vitameatavegamin nor pour it steadily onto the spoon—she calls it "this stuff" and downs it Bowery-style, straight from the bottle. Her shtick deteriorates from "Do you poop out at parties? Are you unpopular?" to "Do you pop out at parties? Are you unpoopular?"

Jess Oppenheimer observed that at the first reading of each new script Ball "didn't know what the hell she was doing." Most scripts were stuffed with stage directions, and the script for "Lucy Does a TV Commercial" was no exception—it had a page and a half of instructions, down to Lucy's winks at the camera. But Ball "took the material to the mat . . . fought with it, examined it, internalized it, and when it reappeared, she owned it."

The tricky task for the show's stage manager, Herb Browar, was to find a real substance to represent Vitameatavegamin that was syrupy yet tasted tolerable to Ball. After a half dozen failed efforts—including honey—Brower found apple pectin at a local health-food store.

The set for the "audition scene" was decorated with bottles of Vitameatavegamin stacked on a table behind a podium where Lucy was to stand, make her pitch, and then demonstrate the product. A sign touting VITAMEATAVEGAMIN: SPOON YOUR WAY TO HEALTH hung on a backdrop. The

Repeated rehearsals
leave her loopy and
unable to spin her spiel
without stumbling.

script originally called for Vitameatavegamin to contain only 11 percent alcohol, so labels printed and placed on all of the prop bottles stated CONTAINS 11% ALCOHOL. But during rehearsals, Ball and the writers decided that it might be funnier if the alcohol content was increased to 23 percent. Since the script didn't call for any close-up shots of the bottles themselves, the prop department didn't bother to reprint the labels.

True to form, in front of the live studio audience, Ball amazed everyone on the staff by nailing the lengthy scene in one take. She even surprised herself. Ball's daughter, Lucie Arnaz, says that it was Ball who requested the show's script clerk (and future *Here's Lucy* director) Maury Thompson sit in on the scene portraying a "script clerk." Ball instructed Thompson to prompt her verbally if she looked over at him. She never did. Writer Madelyn Pugh-Davis says Ball wandered off course only once but knew the material so well she was able to ad-lib, making it even funnier, and then find her way back into the script. Ball, whose

mentor was silent film comedian Buster Keaton, made everything seem fresh, almost improvised.

Over the next five seasons, *I Love Lucy* produced other hilarious and memorable highlights—Lucy and Ethel in the chocolate factory, the birth of Little Ricky, Lucy stomping grapes in Italy, and Lucy baking an enormously long loaf of bread. But beneath the farcical exaggerations, *Lucy* revealed the genuine passions and strains of marriage. Portrayed with a warm heart—Ball made her character lovable despite her mischievousness, and Arnaz infused Ricky with true love for Lucy—the show played strictly for laughs and was never preachy or moralistic. After 179 episodes, Ball and Arnaz decided to end the series.

In the *I Love Lucy* 50th anniversary television special that aired in November 2001 on CBS, fans voted the Vitameatavegamin episode as their all-time favorite *Lucy* moment. *I Love Lucy* still thrives, never once going off the air. The show remains "Tasty, too. Just like candy."

Clockwise from far left: The more Vitameatavegamin she drinks, the loopier she gets. ▪ The original bottle showing 11% alcohol, which was later changed to a whopping 23%. ▪ Lucy tries bread baking. ▪ Stomping grapes in Italy. ▪ Lucy and Ethel at the chocolate factory.

The Ed Sullivan Show

Elvis Debuts

September 9, 1956

Wwhen Elvis Presley appeared on *The Ed Sullivan Show*, the result was what both men hoped for: enormous controversy and enormous TV ratings. And neither popular music nor television would ever be the same.

Every Sunday night at eight o'clock, from 1948 to 1971, millions of Americans faithfully tuned in to *The Ed Sullivan Show* on CBS. From his pulpit as host, Sullivan introduced Americans to all forms of entertainment, from singers and dancers to comedians, jugglers, and acrobats—vaudeville for a television age. Everyone who was anyone—from James Brown to the Beatles, from Richard Pryor to the Muppets—appeared on *Sullivan*.

For all his success, Sullivan was an unlikely television star. He was a former sportswriter and theater columnist for the *New York Daily News* who later

Right: The noise of the fans' screams when Elvis was onstage was deafening. ■ *At his first appearance on* The Ed Sullivan Show, *Elvis drew a record-setting audience of 60 million people.*

worked in radio. When the show first aired, on June 20, 1948, it was called *Toast of the Town*. The comedy team of Dean Martin and Jerry Lewis performed on the debut show, as did Broadway composers Richard Rodgers and Oscar Hammerstein II. The program's name changed to *The Ed Sullivan Show* in 1955.

Television critics loved to skewer Sullivan, usually for his conservative dress, awkward mannerisms, and deadpan delivery, earning him the nickname Great Stone Face. Unlike other variety show hosts, he didn't sing, dance, or tell jokes. "I regret that I'm handicapped by no talent at all," he once said about himself. Sullivan's genius was in identifying and promoting top talent, and he paid handsomely to secure it. He also paid attention to teenagers' obsessions and, in so doing, promoted many rock and roll pioneers.

In 1956 rock and roll music was beginning to surge in popularity among young people, and Elvis Presley had a lot to do with that shift. He recorded hard-edged songs, combining driving rhythm and blues and country influences. At the age of 20, Presley switched from Memphis-based Sun Records to RCA and recorded an extraordinary string of hits—including "Heartbreak Hotel," "Hound Dog," and "Don't Be Cruel." In the process he redefined popular music.

"In 1956," wrote biographer Peter Guralnick, "Elvis Presley burst like a thunderbolt upon a startled nation."

But in the conservative 1950s, Presley's sexually suggestive live performances were both dynamic and jaw-droppingly controversial. He was manically afire onstage. His hip gyrations and pelvic thrusts earned him the nickname Elvis

Presley made his debut on *The Ed Sullivan Show*. Sullivan's producer, Marlo Lewis, flew to Los Angeles to supervise the transcontinental telecast, which originated from CBS Television City in Hollywood.

In August, Sullivan had been in a near-fatal automobile accident outside his country home in Seymour, Connecticut.

the Pelvis. Many considered him immoral. In fact, Sullivan vowed not to have Presley on his show. But he would soon change his tune.

In January 1956, under the shrewd direction of his manager, Colonel Tom Parker, Presley made his first of six national television appearances on *Stage Show*, a Saturday night program hosted by the Dorsey brothers.

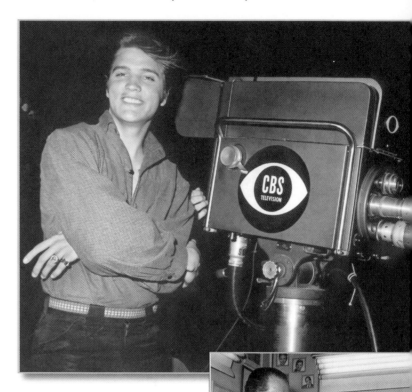

"In 1956 . . . Elvis Presley burst like a thunderbolt upon a startled nation."

Left to right: Elvis greets his fans. ■ With Sullivan before his second appearance. ■ Mugging for the camera. ■ Presley dyed his sandy hair to his trademark jet black before the second show. ■ Presley's appearance with Sullivan opened the doors for other pop music stars, and soon the Rolling Stones and the Beatles followed the King on Ed's stage.

Then he made two appearances on *The Milton Berle Show*. But it was his next appearance, on *The Steve Allen Show*, on Sunday, July 1, 1956, that caught Sullivan's attention. Sullivan on CBS and Allen on NBC aired opposite each other, and Presley's appearance beat Sullivan in the ratings. On Monday, Sullivan scoffed to a reporter, "I don't think Elvis Presley is fit for family viewing," and then he called Colonel Parker. Despite his vow to ignore Presley, Sullivan agreed to pay him the unprecedented sum of $50,000 for three appearances.

On September 9, 1956, while in Hollywood filming his first feature for Twentieth Century Fox, *Love Me Tender*,

He was still recuperating the night of Presley's first appearance, so actor Charles Laughton, star of *Mutiny on the Bounty*, stepped in to host. After "educating" older audience members on Presley's importance in the music business, Laughton introduced Elvis with "And now, away to Hollywood to meet Elvis Presley." Once the teenybopper hysteria subsided, Presley politely thanked his host and humbly admitted, "This is probably the greatest honor that I've ever had in my life." Then Presley and his band launched into hits like "Don't Be Cruel," "Love Me Tender," and "Ready Teddy." Presley teasingly introduced his final song by saying, "Friends, as a great philosopher once said," then shouted, "You ain't nothin' but a hound dog." A record-setting 60 million people, the largest audience in television history to that point, tuned in. The appearance scored a 43.7 Trendex rating, reaching 82.6 percent of television audiences.

Sullivan was back for Presley's second appearance, on October 28, 1956. Before the show, according to biographer Guralnick, Presley dyed his naturally sandy colored hair for the first time, making it his trademark jet black. Sullivan attempted to play along with Presley's bad-boy image. "I can't figure this darned thing out," he said to the audience. "He just does this"—and here Sullivan shook himself—"and everybody yells." Presley and company again performed several numbers, including repeats of "Don't Be Cruel" and "Love Me Tender." This time he

facetiously introduced "Hound Dog" as "one of the saddest songs we've ever heard."

Presley returned to New York for his third and final *Sullivan* appearance on January 6, 1957. However, the controversy over his provocative performing style was growing. Clergy and journalists across the country were lambasting him as "morally insane" and those who promoted him as "culprits guilty of selfish exploitation." Apparently Sullivan grew concerned that Presley's moves were too incendiary and decreed that the cameras shoot the singer only from the waist up. In spite of his precautionary presentation of Presley, after the final number Sullivan thanked the singer by saying, "This is a real decent, fine boy. We've never had a pleasanter experience on our show with a big name than we've had with you. . . . You're thoroughly all right."

Together, *The Ed Sullivan Show* and Elvis Presley built a bridge over the generation gap that existed in pop music. In the months and years to come, such legendary rockers as the Beatles, the Rolling Stones, and the Doors would use that bridge to cross into America's living rooms.

The Dick Van Dyke Show

"That's My Boy?"

September 25, 1963

In 1958, Carl Reiner was already a successful television comedy writer and actor. He had honed his skills as a sketch writer and performer in Broadway revues and on such early groundbreaking television programs as *Your Show of Shows*. So when he created a new series called *Head of the House*, a family-oriented situation comedy about the life of a comedy writer named Rob Petrie, it seemed natural to cast himself in the lead role. Though Reiner shone in the pilot episode and the basic premise was solid, the networks passed. It was fellow actor turned producer-director and Reiner's future partner Sheldon Leonard who delivered the tough news: The show was good but the casting was all wrong. There was something missing. That something turned out to be Dick Van Dyke, aided by his perfectly cast costars:

Left to right: Rob and Laura Petrie with their new baby. ■ The Petries became one of television's most beloved families. ■ In addition to Van Dyke and Moore, the series starred Rose Marie and Morey Amsterdam as Van Dyke's fellow writers.

luminous newcomer Mary Tyler Moore and veteran comic actors Rose Marie and Morey Amsterdam.

Dick Van Dyke is one of the most versatile performers ever to appear on network television. Much as *I Love Lucy* was a perfect vehicle for Lucille Ball, *The Dick Van Dyke Show* was a tailor-made showcase for his unique comic talents, which included his facility as a premiere physical performer. That physicality was the source of one of the most memorable aspects of the show—its rotating opening sequence.

In the series' first season, the opening sequence was a montage—a simple static assemblage of still photographs featuring the show's cast. But heading into the second season, the network executives at CBS were looking for a way to "hook" viewers during the show's first seconds. As the show's producer-writer, it was left up to Carl Reiner to come up with that hook—a job he was not overjoyed to have because he was not con-

vinced anything would work. "Don't do a main title," Reiner initially advised the network. "Just start with the show." They responded, "No, you have to have the main title to let them know what they're watching." In reluctantly acquiescing, Reiner suggested something a little more creative. "Well, the only thing you can do is change the main title every week so the audience will say, 'Hey, what are they gonna do this week?'"

And that led to his simple but compelling solution. The opening would feature Van Dyke's amazing ability for pratfalls. He'd arrive home, stride self-confidently

into the living room, and fall face-first to the floor over a misplaced ottoman. Reiner decided to take the idea a step further. He filmed a second version: Van Dyke looks like he's going to trip but nimbly sidesteps the errant piece of furniture. The "hook" was whether Dick would trip or sidestep. The only person who knew which was going to happen each week was the show's editor, who rotated the clips randomly.

The original ottoman sequences were shot on August 14, 1962, moments after completing that week's regular episode, "The Two Faces of Rob." No one in the cast or crew was terribly excited by the prospect of additional work that evening, especially director John Rich. He had a dinner date and recalls "I was irritated, frankly, about having to shoot this thing." But shoot it they did. The cast was still in costume from that day's episode and Rich put them right to work. The director remembers that getting the shots required not much more than the 20 seconds each opening clip ran, and each was completed in one take. "Dick came in, fell over the thing, and we shot it. And I said, 'That's fine, let's go home.'" That's when Reiner reminded him of the second shot, which the smooth-working cast and crew completed just as expeditiously. "We shot it," Rich remembers, "and I went off on my date. The whole thing took about three minutes." A third variation was filmed after the second season, one in which Van Dyke sidesteps the ottoman, but stumbles and almost falls. It was the least used of the clips.

After five years and 158 episodes, *The Dick Van Dyke Show* produced many memorable moments. But episode number 64, titled "That's My Boy?" draws a near consensus as the episode that provides one of the most memorable moments in the show's history. It was the show that opened the series' third season on September 25, 1963.

Left: In 158 shows, Moore and Van Dyke created some of the most memorable family sitcom episodes in television history. Right: Van Dyke's expressions of shock and embarrassment on discovering that the Peters were black created a classic moment in television comedy. ■ During its five-year run, the show won 16 Emmys.

"That's My Boy?" was the brainchild of the show's newest writers, Bill Persky and Sam Denoff. In fact, it was the idea for that particular show that convinced a bone-weary Carl Reiner to hire the young writing team. "Persky and Denoff . . . really saved my life," Reiner remembers, "because up till then I'd been really alone. I was my own story editor, I had written 40 of the first 60 episodes, and I . . . really needed help."

The premise for "That's My Boy?" was simple, but Reiner recognized immediately that it was perfect to "hang jokes on." The episode is a flashback to the birth of Rob and Laura Petrie's son, Ritchie, and Rob's bizarre notion that the baby they brought home from the hospital was not theirs. Blaming it on a clerical error at the hospital, a frazzled Rob convinces himself that they have the "Peters" baby, not the "Petrie" baby. Laura is just as adamant that their new bundle of joy is, indeed, theirs.

In the segment's finale, Rob calls Mr. and Mrs. Peters,

the couple he thinks has his child, and invites them to his house to settle the question once and for all. Then and only then does Rob give up his wacky idea. When the Peters show up and Rob opens the door, he sees that the couple standing in front of him is . . . black!

Dick Van Dyke's performance in that single moment is one for the ages. In the space of a few heartbeats, he is able to portray Rob's shock, relief, and, finally, his supreme embarrassment. Mr. Peters, who was played by future *Mission Impossible* star Greg Morris, simply watches, savoring the moment.

It was a moment that might not have made it to the TV screen if the show's producer, Sheldon Leonard, had given in to the series' concerned sponsor, Procter and Gamble. The problem, in their eyes, was that some viewers might see Mr. and Mrs. Peters as the butt of the joke. Leonard recalls that the sponsor's representative said, "It's going to look like we're making fun of the black man." To which Leonard replied, "No, it's not! It's going to look like we're making fun of Van Dyke. The black man is smarter, more self-contained. And he has more dignity." The representative seemed to be placated, but shortly before the show was filmed, CBS itself started expressing concerns along the very same lines.

With just a few hours left until showtime, Sheldon Leonard went to battle for his show. This time he made the nervous network a deal—they'd film the show as usual in front of a live audience. If one person in that studio had a problem with the ending, he'd reshoot it at his own expense, any way that CBS wanted.

Needless to say, Leonard did not have to pull his wallet out of his pocket. After an initial gasp, the studio audience began to laugh—and laugh and laugh and laugh some more. It went on so long that Dick Van Dyke says he felt like he was suspended in time. "They would not stop

> # In the space of a few heartbeats, he is able to portray Rob's shock, relief, and, finally, his supreme embarrassment.

laughing," he remembers. "We stood there forever." And then the audience began to applaud. In the end, the laughing and clapping went on for so long that a portion of it had to be edited out to keep the show within its time limit.

There may have been episodes that were more poignant, more slapstick, or more cutting edge, but "That's My Boy?" is generally regarded as *The Dick Van Dyke Show*'s most memorable episode, because it got the show's single biggest reaction from a studio audience in its entire five-season run.

The Fugitive
"The Judgment"

August 29, 1967

It was never a whodunit. From the prologue of the opening episode that aired on September 24, 1963, a transfixed nation of viewers knew who had killed Helen Kimble. They watched as Dr. Richard Kimble returned home from an aimless drive around his Stafford, Indiana, neighborhood after a fight with his wife. They saw the figure of the assailant fleeing from Kimble's home spotlighted in the headlights of the doctor's car as it screeched to a halt. Their eyes zeroed in on the empty sleeve where the figure's right arm should have been, before the mysterious "one-armed" intruder disappeared into the night.

But in the fictional world of Richard Kimble, only he and the one-armed man shared the true story of Helen's death. Kimble was charged and convicted of her murder, but before the electric chair could claim him, he escaped when the train carrying him to his execution derailed.

For the next four years and 120 episodes, David Janssen as Dr. Richard Kimble ran across the television landscape as the star of *The Fugitive*, a unique, groundbreaking series that was the brainchild of television producer Roy Huggins. Each episode was self-contained but, at the same time, part of television's first miniseries, before that word had even been coined.

Every week Kimble found a new job, often a new love, always a new life. In 60 minutes of airtime he would solve the problems of those he encountered, but never his own. Each week, as the law closed in, he would resume his flight, always one step behind the one-armed man, always one step ahead of Lt. Philip Gerard, the officer from whom Kimble had escaped. Gerard had become as obsessed with finding Kimble as Kimble was with catching up to his one-armed tormentor, whose name in the series was Fred Johnson.

Right: Moving from town to town by bus, train, car, and plane, the fugitive kept one step ahead of the law.

There were similarities between the show and the classic fugitive story *Les Misérables*, and also with the highly publicized 1950s case in which Dr. Samuel Sheppard was convicted of murdering his wife, a charge that was later overturned by the U.S. Supreme Court. But Huggins said that Kimble had no links to either Jean Valjean in *Les Misérables* or to Sheppard.

Huggins had made his mark in television in the late 1950s by producing western series such as *Cheyenne* and *Maverick*. With the western on the wane in the early 1960s, Huggins was looking for a way to bring the central appeal of that format into modern times, to offer a hero who could move from town to town in episode after episode, clean up Dodge, and then ride off into the sunset.

That was acceptable back in the 19th century. Huggins wondered how he could make such wanderlust believable in a character while still convincing the audience he was a responsible, stable person worthy of their time and support. The only way to do that, Huggins decided, was to put his character in a position where he was forced to be constantly on the move.

In his original proposal for *The Fugitive*, Huggins referred to the western hero as "a man without roots, without obligations, without fixed goals, without anxiety about his place in the order of things." That was Kimble, moving on and on, working as a bartender, then as a sail maker, then as a sculptor's model and on to fish hatchery worker. Along the way, Kimble bumped into a who's who of Hollywood, from Bruce Dern to Leslie Nielsen to Ron Howard to Carroll O'Connor, all playing supporting roles in the show's four-year run.

The biggest question about most television series is How long will it last? Because of its unusual nature, there was a second question for *The Fugitive:* How will it end? Will Kimble ever catch the one-armed man? And if he does, how will Kimble prove the one-armed man's guilt?

The decision to cancel *The Fugitive* after four seasons was made not because of poor ratings, but because of the

poor health of its star. Required to be in nearly every scene, Janssen was suffering from an old high school football injury. By the middle of the fourth season, the physical demands of the show were too painful, and Janssen wanted out. Producer Quinn Martin felt the loyal audience deserved closure to the series, but he later questioned his decision. Martin worried that the rerun potential would be hurt because a climax to *The Fugitive* might dull interest in earlier episodes. But creator Roy Huggins always believed that the show should come to a natural conclusion.

There was no doubt that Dr. Kimble would be vindicated. "Richard Kimble had, for four years, been chasing the one-armed man," said George Eckstein, who wrote the final script along with Michael Zagor. "If he had been chasing the wrong man, it would have been a joke. He would have looked like a jerk. So it had to be the one-armed man who did it."

Although the destination was assured, the route didn't have to be direct. Eckstein and Zagor came up with a script worthy of the grand finale, a two-parter entitled "The Judgment." In the first part, Fred Johnson is arrested in Los Angeles for robbery. Gerard flies in to question him and Kimble is drawn to L.A. by the news. But a mysterious benefactor bails Johnson out. To his horror, Kimble discovers the name on the bail receipt is Len Taft, his brother-in-law in Indiana. Before he can investigate further, Kimble is captured by Gerard.

In the concluding episode, Johnson returns to Stafford where he confronts the real man who bailed him out using Taft's name, Stafford city planning commissioner Lloyd Chandler. Chandler had been in the Kimble house the night of the murder and had witnessed the crime but was

too paralyzed by fear to act. A war hero, Chandler never came forward in Kimble's defense because that would have destroyed his own reputation. Johnson blackmails Chandler, demanding that he bring $50,000 to a nearby amusement park. Chandler goes there, not with money, but with a gun to kill Johnson. Kimble and Gerard, learning the whole story from Chandler's wife, rush to the park where Kimble and Johnson engage in a death struggle at the top of a tower. Johnson finally confesses to Kimble that indeed he had killed Kimble's wife. Finally, with Kimble about to be shot by Johnson, Gerard fires a shot that kills the one-armed man. A tearful Chandler agrees to testify that he saw Johnson murder Helen Kimble.

According to writer Eckstein, filming the final dramatic sequence was fraught with logistical problems. An abandoned amusement park was chosen to allow the characters to be isolated. While the story takes place in Indiana, the only amusement park available in Hollywood was Pacific Ocean Park, which was surrounded on three sides by the Pacific Ocean. "Shooting around that ocean was not easy to do," says Eckstein. "It took a lot of ingenuity on the part of the director to avoid seeing what was three-quarters of the background in that sequence." Eckstein still laments over having the struggle between Kimble and Johnson take place at the top of the observation tower. "Why anybody being chased would run up a 40-foot tower I have no idea. That's a dramatic convenience that still rings false to me, but theatrically it worked." As for the decision to have Gerard kill

Left to right: In the concluding episode, Lt. Gerard and Kimble team up to catch the one-armed man. ■ Kimble chases the one-armed murderer through an amusement park and up a tall tower, where Gerard shoots him before he can kill Kimble.

Johnson, Eckstein says that was so Gerard could have closure, too. "This way it wasn't vigilante justice. It wasn't Kimble taking the law into his own hands. I think we would have received some flack had we had Kimble shoot Johnson; Gerard is an officer of the law and fully credentialed."

Narrator William Conrad spoke the final words of the series as Kimble walked out of court a free man. "Tuesday, August 29th," intoned Conrad, referring not only to Kimble's release, but the day the episode was airing, "the day the running stopped."

Those words were heard by 72 percent of those watching television across the nation that night, and Eckstein believes that it's a tribute to David Janssen. "He was more or less the consummate television actor. He projected this

"Why anybody being chased would run up a 40-foot tower I have no idea. That's a dramatic convenience that still rings false to me, but theatrically it worked."

decency, this vulnerability, and strength all at the same time. I think the audience really identified with him and that's what got us the share."

The Fugitive: "The Judgment" became the highest-rated single episode in television history, a distinction it held for 13 seasons—until somebody shot J.R.

All in the Family
"Sammy's Visit"

Right: The Bunker family's generation gap and its confrontations with the new feminism embodied the cultural shifts of the times.

February 19, 1972

Jungle bunny. Spade. Hebe. Spic. Mick. Chink. And, of course, dumb Polack. Dialogue never heard in any television sitcom household until the Bunkers moved into the CBS lineup on January 12, 1971.

Inspired by a British TV comedy called *Till Death Do Us Part*, about a middle-aged hotheaded lout, Alf Garnett, and his sharp-tongued wife, Else, veteran television writer-producer Norman Lear purchased the rights to the U.K. hit, then combined it with his own family experiences to create his new series. Lear's father, Herman, used to tell his wife to "stifle yourself" and even called Norman "the laziest white man I ever saw."

The last name originally given to Lear's new TV family was

By making them a source of laughter, we hope to show—in a mature fashion—just how absurd they are." Then viewers heard the sound of a toilet flush, and *All in the Family* was off and running. It was a funny, outrageous, and incisive show made for its time, when the country was undergoing cultural shifts of seismic proportions.

Justice, making the show's first title *Justice for All*, then *Those Were the Days*. Mickey Rooney was Lear's first choice to play the show's bigoted patriarch, but Rooney was scared off by the controversy and doubted the show would last. Carroll O'Connor, as liberal as Archie was conservative, grabbed the opportunity, but he too was certain the show would flop. ABC shot the pilot but soon got cold feet and scrapped the project altogether.

Looking to shed its *Lassie, Mayberry R.F.D., Beverly Hillbillies* identity, CBS leapt at the opportunity. Retitled *All in the Family*, the revolutionary sitcom was ready to debut January 12, 1971. In a preemptive move to reduce the expected negative public backlash, CBS began the episode with a disclaimer, stating that *All in the Family* "seeks to throw a humorous spotlight on our frailties, prejudices, and concerns.

The show became as much about family themes—the generation gap, love and domestic strife, living with in-laws—as about hot-button topics. But it was the taboo subjects that ignited it, and everything—religion, feminism, menopause, miscarriage, rape, impotence, homosexuality, and political issues like the Vietnam War and President Richard Nixon—seemed fair game. O'Connor and Jean Stapleton, who played Archie's loving yet long-suffering wife, Edith, were both accomplished stage and screen actors, and their chemistry was magical. O'Connor and Rob Reiner, who portrayed long-haired son-in-law Michael "Meathead" Stivic, and Sally Struthers, who played Archie's adoring daughter, Gloria, proved a perfectly incendiary combination.

By its second season, *All in the Family* was the show America was talking about. Archie's prejudice often prompted liberal critics and black leaders, including the head of the Urban League, to complain that bigots laughed with lovable Archie, not at him. But many blacks, including Sammy Davis Jr., who praised it for "exposing some of the ills of today's society," loved the show.

Davis, who scheduled nightclub appearances around watching *All in the Family*, began lobbying for a guest appearance. "Sammy Davis not only approached me, he pestered me," says Lear of his longtime friend. "He adored the show from the very beginning. He would call all the time. 'I've got to do the show, Norman. I've got to do the show.'"

Lear resisted, uncomfortable with upsetting the series' delicate balance. Rather than cram "Mr. Wonderful" into an unrealistic character part, the writers figured out a way for Davis to play himself.

"He hadn't given up the job on the loading dock, but Archie was picking up some extra money driving a cab part-time. Sammy gets in the cab. And then conveniently, too conveniently, perhaps," Lear admits, "Sammy leaves his briefcase in the cab and has to hunt down the cabdriver."

No other episode in the show's history dealt more bluntly with Archie's racism. "We knew we had a lot of comic ingredients," Lear says. "Archie Bunker and a black man. Archie Bunker and a black man who happens to be a celebrity. Archie Bunker and a black man who's a celebrity and has a glass eye. And he's Jewish. You know, it was amazing."

Sally Struthers recalls how excited the cast was when Davis joined them for the first read-through of the script. "Sammy Davis Jr. showed up at rehearsal with gifts for

Left to right: Archie gives Sammy Davis Jr. a ride in his cab. ■ Before Davis's visit, Archie warns the family not to mention Sammy's glass eye. ■ Archie pontificates about racial prejudice.

everyone. He brought us gold necklaces; there were presents every day. He was so generous and so funny, and he was our best audience; even in the scenes he wasn't in, he would sit and watch and laugh at us as we were rehearsing. It was such a happy week on that show."

And so, on February 19, 1972, Sammy Davis Jr. left his briefcase in Archie's cab and came to 704 Hauser Street to retrieve it. The visit was a watershed, grabbing new headlines for the hit series and crackling with dialogue that was risqué even by the show's standards. Archie calls Davis "the greatest credit to his race." Davis, deadpan, responds, "I'm sure you've done some good for yours, too."

Fearful "the dingbat" will strike again, before Davis's arrival Archie cautions Edith not to mention his glass eye. "Maybe the biggest laugh I know in television," Lear says,

"is when Archie tells Edith not mention his glass eye. Do not mention his eye. Do not mention his eye. And then Archie asks Sammy when he's serving him some coffee: 'Now, Mr. Davis . . . do you take cream and sugar in your eye?' That comes right out of character."

And, according to Lear, no one took the joke better than Sammy Davis Jr. "You have to remember that Sammy Davis spent years on the stage with Frank Sinatra and Dean Martin. So he heard all of the short black jokes. All of the Seeing Eye dog jokes. All of the Jewish black jokes. So it was no surprise to him, or no shock in any event, to see a script that alluded to the same things."

Captive in the Bunker house until his briefcase is delivered from the cab company, Davis is dazed by his armchair summit with Archie, which yields one outrageously bigoted notion after another: "I think that if God had meant for us to be together, he'd have put us together. But look what he done. He put you over in Africa, and put the rest of us in all the white countries." "Well," Davis offers, "he must've told 'em where we were because somebody came and got us." And when Archie asks Davis point-blank if he seems prejudiced, Davis responds, "Why, if you were prejudiced, you would have called me nigger or coon. Not you. You came right out and called me colored."

Ultimately, Davis exacts his revenge. When Archie's friend Munson finally arrives with the briefcase, he asks if he can take a picture of Sammy. Davis agrees on one condition, that he be allowed to pose with "my friend Archie." Davis stands next to Archie, instructing Munson to take the shot at the count of three. On three, Davis turns and plants

a kiss on Archie's cheek, transforming Archie's grin into a jumble of horror and confusion. "The genesis of the idea of kissing Archie was Sammy," Lear reveals. "It's probably the

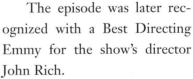

On three, Davis turns and plants a kiss on Archie's cheek, transformng Archie's grin into a jumble of horror and confusion.

most famous kiss in television history." "Carroll O'Connor had to stand there," Struthers recalls, "stand there and just look around with his eyes, and the audience could imagine four million things he was thinking or wanting to say. I think that was one of the longest recorded laughs in television history from a live audience. People couldn't contain themselves."

The episode was later recognized with a Best Directing Emmy for the show's director John Rich.

All in the Family ran nine seasons, although Gloria and Mike moved to California before the last one. After Stapleton left, O'Connor continued for four more years with *Archie Bunker's Place*. Television's most influential show paved the way for spinoffs like *Maude* and *The Jeffersons*, each dealing with race, sex, and other issues as never before. *All in the Family* changed the conventions of situation comedies, and changed the way America looked at television.

The Brady Bunch

"The Subject Was Noses"

Right: Carol and Alice with some of the kids on the kitchen set. ■ Clockwise from top left: Marcia, Cindy, Jan, Bobby, Peter, and Greg in the first season.

February 9, 1973

During its five-year run on ABC, from 1969 to 1974, *The Brady Bunch* never cracked the Nielsen Top 20. Yet the sitcom about a blended family—her three girls and his three boys—has fixed itself as a cornerstone of pop culture.

There's no numerical reason why *The Brady Bunch* should be remembered, much less celebrated with a never-ending stream of books, televised reunions, campy live reenactments, and satirical Hollywood movies. *TV Guide* panned its premiere episode as a "mishmash," and it fared only modestly in the ratings.

The show debuted on ABC on September 26, 1969, a month after Woodstock, and ran for 117 episodes, through August 30, 1974, and Richard Nixon's resignation. This wasn't exactly the wholesome 1950s. But while adult viewers began tuning in to more realistic and sophisticated shows, like *All in the Family* and

The show's opening credits, with a tic-tac-toe board and catchy theme performed by the Peppermint Trolley Company, stand out perhaps as much as any episode. But among regular episodes, "The Subject Was Noses," which originally aired February 9, 1973, has become a classic, particularly for Marcia's "Oh, my nose!" flashback.

Marcia has a typical *Brady Bunch* problem—Doug, the school's handsome football star, whom she deems "far-out"—asks her to the dance. She says yes, but she already has a date with Charley, the quintessential nice guy. When Marcia poses her predicament to her older brother, Greg, he teaches her a

> A sizable young audience seemed to want, even need, an unthreatening, reassuring view of life.

*M*A*S*H,* a sizable young audience seemed to want, even need, an unthreatening, reassuring view of life.

As societal problems and cultural gaps grew more intractable, *The Brady Bunch* appeared to provide a perfect way to restore childhood innocence once a week. Like the equally unrealistic shows of earlier generations, it existed in a cocoon, where there was plenty of money, the issues were trivial, and Father, and Mother, still knew best.

Originally titled *Yours and Mine*, the show was created by Sherwood Schwartz, who also created *Gilligan's Island*. According to Schwartz's son, and the show's associate producer, Lloyd Schwartz, "Over half the episodes that occurred on *Brady* came, almost word for word, from the Schwartz household. One of the criticisms of *Brady Bunch* has always been, you know, 'Families aren't like that.' Well," Schwartz mused, "maybe your family wasn't . . ."

Schwartz interviewed 464 children for the six kids' roles—Greg (Barry Williams), Marcia (Maureen McCormick), Peter (Christopher Knight), Jan (Eve Plumb), Bobby (Michael Lookinland), and Cindy (Susan Olsen)—which ranged from age seven to 14 in the first season. The roles of Alice the maid (Ann B. Davis), Mike (Robert Reed), and Carol (Florence Henderson) were cast afterward—with pre-*French Connection* Gene Hackman reportedly among those considered for the father figure.

dishonest way out, the trick of saying "something suddenly came up," which Charley accepts passively.

But then Peter's poorly passed football clobbers Marcia. "Oh, my nose," she cries. Her dreams of romance with Doug recede as her nose swells. Marcia sits in her room mortified, reliving the incident again and again in slow motion. BAM! "Oh, my nose!" BAM! "Oh, my nose!" BAM! "Oh, my nose!"

The job of plunking actress Maureen McCormick in the nose fell to associate producer Schwartz. "Irving and Joe were the two propmen, and they made this kind of spongy football," Schwartz explains. "I said, 'Maureen, stand over there,' and I hit her with the ball. It was one shot. And I hate to admit it, but that might be my biggest claim to fame. It certainly gets the most reaction." Schwartz laughs.

"I was actually so freaked out, because at first when they brought it out I thought it was a real football," McCormick admits. "It looked like a real football. And, back then, they didn't have Nerf balls."

Marcia tries keeping her painful, albeit temporary,

imperfection hidden, but Doug accidentally spots her swollen nose and immediately tells her that "something suddenly came up" for him on Saturday night. Marcia has learned her lesson.

According to Schwartz, "It's a very traditional *Brady* episode, where vanity plays a part. When someone is vain, what you do is puncture that and, in this case, flatten that."

So when her nose heals—"Now the world can look me in the face and I can look back"—and Doug reasks her out, Marcia milks the episode's catchphrase, telling him "something suddenly came up," and comes clean with Charley. "It was really a classic episode because it did what *Brady* always tried to do, which was teach a little lesson," says Schwartz.

Although the series was canceled in August 1974, the Bradys never really faded away. Even while the original show was on the air, ABC ran *The Brady Kids*, a Saturday morning cartoon, for two years. Later came the short-lived *Brady Bunch Hour* variety show. Then a successful TV movie, *The Brady Girls Get Married*, followed by the 1981 series *The Brady Brides*, which flopped after only two months. But the clan bounced back with the 1988 hit movie *A Very Brady Christmas*. In the 1990s the Bradys were reinterpreted by others with surprising success. *The Real Live Brady Bunch* was a campy hit onstage, featuring look-alike actors reenacting various episodes. Then came the box-office hit *The Brady Bunch Movie*, a parody with the family happily and obliviously stuck in the '70s while surrounded by the real-world styles of the 1990s.

What TV classic has an afterlife like that?

Left to right: The family that plays together stays together was a popular Brady theme. ▪ *Christopher Knight, just outside the closed set.* ▪ *Between takes.* ▪ *Story lines highlighted all of the usual teenage problems.* ▪ *The cast members as they appeared in 1974 when the show was canceled.*

Saturday Night Live
The Early Years

1975 to 1980

Right: Lorne Michaels at a 1993 press conference. ■ *The original* SNL *cast in 1975: Chevy Chase, John Belushi, Gilda Radner, Laraine Newman, Garrett Morris, Jane Curtin, and Dan Aykroyd.*

The mere mention of Land Sharks, Coneheads, and the Samurai, or catchphrases like "Cheeseburger! Cheeseburger! Cheeseburger!" "Jane, you ignorant slut," and "We're two wild and crazy guys!" triggers a rush of memories for an entire generation of TV viewers.

Saturday Night Live rose from its wasteland of network television time slots to become a pop culture phenomenon and in the process caused a seismic shift in the landscape of television comedy-variety the likes of which hadn't been seen since Sid Caesar's *Your Show of Shows* went on the air in 1950.

In its more than a quarter of a century on television, and after more than twice that many writer and cast changes, *SNL* has cycled from hip to hokey, hilarious to ho-hum, bland to brilliant. "Over the years, it's taken lots of different shapes, depending upon the strength of the cast or whether something really interesting is happening in politics, music, or not," says *SNL* creator and producer Lorne Michaels. "I think at the beginning, we were doing the show for ourselves; the fact that we were making it up as we went along was thrilling."

The consensus among fans and critics alike is that the show was at its best and its most influential with the original cast in the mid to late 1970s, when it transformed television, societal mores, and America's social calendar for Saturday night.

Before *SNL* hit the air in 1975, the very notion of a comedy-variety show seemed like a quaint anachronism. And the idea of a program for young people on Saturday night seemed patently absurd. But NBC took a chance on the show's 30-year-old creator, Michaels, who had written for *Laugh-In* and had just won an Emmy for writing a Lily Tomlin special. "Because it was on Saturday night, and because research had shown that people wouldn't be home on Saturday nights, it was a very low-stakes game," recalls Michaels. "There was this sort of intoxicating freedom. We were so completely in the moment that it was probably the most exciting time in my life."

While NBC was pushing him to cast network-approved talent like impressionist Rich Little, Michaels was aiming for an edgier show, so he turned instead to comic performers from young improvisational troupes like Chicago's Second City and Los Angeles's Groundlings, who wouldn't rely on old TV tricks and clichés.

Among his first hires were Gilda Radner and Dan Aykroyd, both of whom Michaels knew from his work in comedy theater in his native Toronto. Then he brought in Laraine Newman. "We had worked together on the Tomlin special, and I was crazy about her," recalls Michaels. He found actors Chevy Chase and John Belushi performing in a sketch comedy revue called *National Lampoon's Lemmings*. Although Belushi considered television "beneath him," he was intrigued by Michaels's grand experiment and agreed to try it out. Actress Jane Curtin and actor Garrett Morris rounded out the cast. "I think for most of the cast it was their first job in television," says Michaels, prompting him to name his new troupe the Not Ready for Prime Time Players.

The show, originally titled *Saturday Night* to differentiate it from a new ABC series called *Saturday Night Live with Howard Cosell*, debuted October 11, 1975, from NBC's

Studio 8H in Rockefeller Plaza. When Cosell's show was canceled, the NBC show appropriated the word *Live*.

Michaels and the network butted heads from the start, beginning with Michaels's choice for the debut show's guest host, George Carlin. Carlin, the controversial comedian known for his drug-laced humor and infamous "seven words you can't say on television" routine, had a standard stage attire of jeans and a T-shirt. When the NBC brass said his wardrobe choice didn't befit a network show, Carlin wore his T-shirt under a suit.

A wide range of actors, musicians, and newsmakers have followed in Carlin's footsteps, from Steve Martin to Hugh Hefner,

Glenn Close to Nancy Kerrigan, Rev. Jesse Jackson to Ralph Nader, and Frank Zappa to the Rolling Stones.

The buzz on *SNL* was big, and it quickly became the hippest show on television. Suddenly everyone was making sure to be home by 11:30 on Saturday night to see the lampooning of icons like Julia Child (blood gushing from her finger, "Oh, now I've done it, I've cut the dickens out of my finger!") and Barbara Walters ("Hewwo. This is Baba Wawa"), commercial parodies for products like Quarry cereal ("Contains no preservatives, no additives, no artificial flavoring—because Quarry isn't grown, it's mined"), the Super Bass-O-Matic blender ("You'll never have to scale, cut, or gut again"), or Little Chocolate Donuts ("Donuts of champions!"), as well as a raft of break-out *SNL* characters like Theodoric of York the medieval barber, the sharp-tongued consumer affairs reporter Roseanne Roseannadana, and the oversexed, always cruising and swinging Festrunk Brothers.

From the beginning, world leaders and politicians were in the crosshairs of *SNL*'s political parodies. In addition to his regular role as the anchor of the news spoof "Weekend Update," Chevy Chase began an *SNL* tradition when he

created a self-styled version of President Gerald Ford. A master of physical comedy, Chase was inspired when Ford was caught on camera tripping down the last couple of steps from Air Force One. "Chevy made absolutely no effort to *look* like Gerald Ford," says Michaels. "He was playing an attitude. He just said, 'I'm the president.' And there are very few people who can pull that off."

In one of the show's classic political parodies, which aired September 18, 1976, Chase, playing a bumbling incumbent President Ford, squared off against his challenger, Governor Jimmy Carter, played by Dan Aykroyd. On the issue of abortion, Chase as Ford affirms, "I support a

constitutional amendment allowing the states to decide their own abortion laws. This would allow a woman who wants an abortion to travel to another state." Aykroyd as Carter rebuts confidently, "I think my stance on abortion is perfectly ambiguous and ill-defined, and see no reason to elaborate any further." After Chase spills a pitcher of water, he falls face forward over the podium, bringing the debates to a halt.

Chase left *SNL* after the first season, and actor Bill Murray, another Second City alum, filled the opening in 1977. Murray was responsible for creating a number of memorable characters. Among them was the noogie-crazed Todd DiLaMuca, who along with Gilda Radner's creation

Left to right: Aykroyd plays Julia Child. ■ News anchor Curtin reacts to Radner's guest commentator Roseanne Roseannadana. ■ Chase in his hilarious impression of Gerald Ford, with Ford's real press secretary, Ron Nessen. ■ Bill Murray, Steve Martin, and Gilda Radner as Nerds.

of the ever-sniffling Lisa Loopner introduced the Nerds, in a show that aired on January 28, 1978. Todd, who lovingly refers to Lisa as Four Eyes, and Lisa, who adoringly calls Todd Pizza Face, reminded everyone of what it was like to suffer through adolescence. Murray and Radner, who were actually engaged in a turbulent affair at the time, portrayed the awkward teens with affection and comic flair. "There was nothing self-conscious about those characters," says Michaels. "They *were* the characters, and the sweetness that's there is, in addition to being obviously very funny, the affection that they clearly have for each other and for the characters."

The Nerds skits were mostly written by Michaels's ex-wife, Rosie Shuster, and Anne Beatts. Jane Curtin played Lisa's mother, Enid, who loved making egg salad—"that and ironing contour sheets"—and constantly struggled to keep everyone's hormones in check.

One memorable Nerds skit involved Enid's old, beloved Norge refrigerator. The reliable Norge has gone on the fritz, and when the repairman, played by Aykroyd, bends down to take a look, his low-riding pants give Lisa, Todd, and the audience more than an eyeful of his backside. Todd, howling in adolescent hysterics, remarks, "Yeah, the moon came out surprisingly early." To which Lisa replies in disgust, "Todd, no wise cracks!"

The success of *SNL* brought attention and opportunity to the cast. In 1978 John Belushi made his motion picture debut for director John Landis. He played a degenerate frat boy named Bluto Blutarsky in the raucous comedy about the goings-on at a bad-boy fraternity called *Animal House*. The movie premiered on June 1, 1978, and quickly became a launchpad for Belushi's big-screen career. About that time Belushi and Aykroyd had parlayed their Blues Brothers characters into a successful recording act, with a sold-out tour and a number one debut album, *Briefcase Full of Blues*, and a Blues Brothers movie went into production in 1979. *Saturday Night Live* was no longer important to the two original cast members, and NBC let them out of their contracts early.

By 1980 all the original Not Ready for Prime Time

And that maybe it'll work again next week. So you stay focused on next week, because that's where the best chance of redemption for the past week will appear."

Saturday Night Live launched the careers of dozens of performers and turned improvisation into an institution on late-night TV.

> "Sometimes the things you thought were remarkable turn out to be flat. The things that you had underestimated—explode. And when it works it's a miracle."

Left to right: Belushi's killer bees. ▪ Belushi and Aykroyd created the independently successful Blues Brothers. ▪ Aykroyd's classic, the Bass-O-Matic.

Players had moved on, and so had Michaels. But he returned in 1985 as the driving creative force for the longest running and highest rated late-night program in television history. Despite the show's ebbs and flows in popularity, for Michaels it's all about *this week's* show. "I hope that it's as good as I would like it to be on Saturday. It probably won't be, 'cause I don't think I've ever left the studio going, 'Well, this time we got everything.' I don't always feel we're ready to go on, but we don't go on because it's ready, we go on because it's 11:30. Sometimes the things you thought were remarkable turn out to be flat. The things that you had underestimated—explode. And when it works it's a miracle. And when it doesn't, you try and remember that at one point or another it did work.

Dallas
"Who Done It?"

Left to right: J.R. and Sue Ellen's marriage was tempestuous, to say the least. ■ Larry Hagman as the villainous Texas oilman. ■ The Ewing family.

November 21, 1980

*D*allas wasn't among the most popular programs of the 1980s by accident. Its weekly displays of opulence and excess fit the mood of the decade like a diamond-studded boot.

Dallas told the story of a Texas oil family, the Ewings, who lived on a magnificent and sprawling ranch called South Fork, just outside Dallas. South Fork actually existed in two places: the real ranch, where most of the exterior scenes were shot, was located in Plano, Texas; the interior of the house was on a soundstage at MGM Studios in Culver City, California.

The show was essentially a soap opera, a melodramatic genre popular during the day but not at night, at least since the cancellation of *Peyton Place* in the late 1960s. The show was panned as being "dull and contrived" by the show business newspaper *Variety*.

The series starred Larry Hagman as J. R. Ewing. J.R., one of three brothers, was the ruthless, conniving, and womanizing head of the family business. He and his wife, Sue Ellen (Linda Gray); his parents, Jock (Jim Davis) and Ellie (Barbara Bel Geddes); his brother Bobby (Patrick Duffy); and Bobby's wife, Pamela (Victoria Principal), all lived at the ranch. And the Ewings had enemies to battle, a rival oil family named Barnes.

The show did not begin as a true serial. Originally, each episode wrapped up by the closing credits and viewers

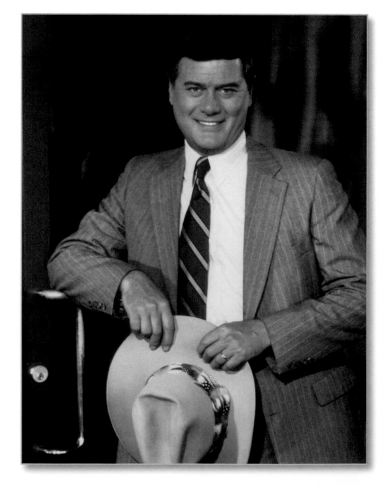

did not have to watch every week to keep up with the plots. But by the end of the second season, there were an estimated 40 characters, and story arcs began to stretch out over several episodes.

By the time the second season ended, *Dallas* had settled into its Friday night time slot and the Nielsen Top 10, drawing 30 to 40 million devoted viewers every week. As a result of *Dallas*'s popularity, CBS asked the producers for two additional episodes. The only problem was that the producers had no idea what to do in the extra two hours. According to *Dallas* writer Loraine Despres, "They were sitting around the office, and they said, 'What do we do? Let's shoot J.R. We'll figure out who shot him over the summer.'" It was Loraine's job to write the whodunit episode.

Initially Hagman thought the idea lacked originality. He wanted his character to step into an elevator shaft in the Ewing oil building and plunge 15 stories. It's rumored that

to shoot himself. It was just done by everybody and their cousin. And that was really fun," says Crosby.

The question "Who shot J.R.?" became ubiquitous through the summer and fall of 1980, causing an international sensation. *Dallas* was a popular program all over the world, with an estimated global audience of 350 million in 57 countries. "I was shooting a miniseries in England that summer," says Crosby. "The 'Who shot J.R.?' mania was even greater in England than it was here [in the United States]. It was really outrageous. England shut down on Friday nights."

Time and *People* magazines ran cover stories. Oddsmakers created betting lines for characters who might have pulled the trigger. In fact, when then-President Jimmy

"The 'Who shot J.R.?' mania was even greater in England than it was here [in the United States]. It was really outrageous. England shut down on Friday nights."

a suicide attempt by Sue Ellen was also discussed, with J.R. accidentally drinking the mixture of alcohol and barbiturates she had prepared for herself.

The season ended with two shots being fired at J.R. in the dark, assailant unknown. The producers were adamant about keeping the identity of the culprit a secret. "They were very clear that this was not going to be something that would get out," explains Mary Crosby, who played Kristin Shepard, J.R.'s devious sister-in-law, sultry mistress, and assailant. "So when they filmed me shooting him, everybody got to shoot Larry. The hairdressers got to shoot him, the makeup artist got to shoot him, the writers, and the producers. Larry got

Left to right: The gun that Kristin used to shoot J.R. ▪ J.R. with mistress Kristin Shepard (played by Mary Crosby), who pulled the trigger. ▪ J.R. recuperates with Sue Ellen after the shooting.

Carter arrived in Texas for a campaign fund-raiser, he said, "I came to Dallas to find out confidentially who shot J.R. If any of you could let me know that, I could finance the whole campaign this fall."

There were off-camera machinations as well. For one thing, an actors' strike that summer delayed shooting of the fall television season. Hagman was also causing a stir, threatening to leave the show if he wasn't paid what he considered a fair wage for being the star of a prime-time hit. Reports circulated that producers began considering actor Robert Culp as a replacement for Hagman. They were prepared to say that J.R. had been shot in the face and would have explained his new look as the result of plastic surgery.

The first episode of the delayed season—titled "Who Done It?"—aired on Friday, November 21, 1980. Around the country, restaurants, theaters, and other public places sat near empty as 80 million Americans tuned in to get the answer. As everyone now knows, J.R. was shot by Kristin, his sister-in-law with whom he had an affair. At the time it was the highest rated single episode in television history, since topped by the series finale of *M*A*S*H*.

The "Who shot J.R.?" cliff-hanger was the high-water mark for *Dallas*, though the show eventually ran for thirteen years and was the highest rated show of the year three times.

Dallas was an innovative and influential program that spawned the hit spin-off *Knots Landing* and a host of soapy imitators, like *Falcon Crest* and *Dynasty* and the youth-oriented *Beverly Hills 90210* and *Melrose Place*. Television staples from *Hill Street Blues* through *thirtysomething* to *ER* might not have been possible had *Dallas* not been successful with stories that took place over several episodes, even whole seasons. Still, it is the cliff-hanger that remains *Dallas*'s true legacy.

Dallas

M*A*S*H
"Goodbye, Farewell, and Amen"

*Left to right: The cast prepares to go home. ■ The Colonel, B.J., Margaret, and Father Mulcahy in a typical M*A*S*H combat pose. ■ Alan Alda's Hawkeye combined playful cynicism with male vulnerability as it had never been portrayed on television before.*

February 28, 1983

Throughout its history, television has dealt with the subject of war—the dramas, the disasters, the tears, even the laughter. But no series conveyed the complexity of those mixed emotions better—or for longer—than *M*A*S*H*. The show debuted on CBS September 17, 1972, and it ventured into territory where few sitcoms dare tread. For 11 seasons and 251 episodes, the bawdy and bloody comedy told the stories of the dedicated yet eccentric corps of doctors, nurses, and staff of the 4077th, and their struggle to keep their humor and humanity in the midst of the inhuman condition of war.

As often as not, the stories were drawn from real life. "I probably interviewed two or three hundred doctors who had served in Korea," said Burt Metcalfe, who over the 11 years of the show wrote, produced, or directed many episodes, including the finale. "It was a very interesting process and enormously helpful. The doctors would go on for hours because it was so cathartic for them. At a medical reunion of one of these units in Chicago, a doctor came up to me and he said, 'I just want to thank you because you've made me a hero to my family. I am somehow like Hawkeye,' and he was very grateful for that," said Metcalfe.

Before television, *M*A*S*H* was a novel written by Richard Hornberger and then a 1970 Oscar-nominated film directed by Robert Altman. Following the movie's success, William Self, head of Twentieth Century Fox, handed *M*A*S*H* to producer Gene Reynolds and veteran comedy writer Larry Gelbart to turn into a series, with the promise that *M*A*S*H* would be an irreverent mix of comedy and drama.

In the novel, men joke, drink, womanize, grab for power, and undercut authority to survive the horrors around them. Gelbart juxtaposed all that with the carnage and the Army's bureaucratic lunacy, creating an antiwar series. Amid the ensemble cast, Alan Alda's Hawkeye Pierce emerged as the face of the show, mixing a Groucho Marx flare for playful sarcasm and innuendo with a vulnerability rarely seen before in a male television lead. Alda once wrote that the show tried to "explore compassion and . . . rage against death and pain."

M*A*S*H finished 46th in the ratings its first season. The next season CBS moved the show to Saturday, between two other adult-themed comedies, *All in the Family* and *The Mary Tyler Moore Show*. It took off, finishing nine of the next 10 seasons in the ratings Top 10.

But even while the characters continued evolving, the years eventually sapped the show of its comic edge—story lines grew thinner, laughs often felt forced, and moralizing and political correctness crept in. "As the material began to dry up," confided Metcalfe, "we decided we'd get out when we were still on top." So Alda and his fellow actors David Ogden Stiers, Loretta Swit, and Mike Farrell reportedly voted to quit

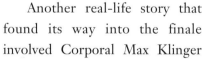

silently. Suddenly a baby belonging to a Korean refugee woman begins to whimper. Responding to Hawkeye's scolding, the refugee smothers her baby to save everyone else. Though Hawkeye eventually returns to the 4077th, he remains jittery, feeling, he says, "up to my ankles in panic" during surgery.

Among the strongest subplots is the one that involves the erudite Dr. Winchester's inadvertent capture of a rag-tag bunch of Chinese musicians, to whom he teaches Mozart during their temporary internment at the 4077th. With the war finally ending, the prisoners are trucked off, only to be killed in the last gasps of battle. Watching the flutist die, Winchester sees classical music—his sole sanctuary throughout the war—irrevocably stained with blood. The Mozart piece, Quintet for Clarinet and Strings, became classical radio's most requested selection after the airing of the finale.

Another real-life story that found its way into the finale involved Corporal Max Klinger

Left to right: The final episode opens with Hawkeye confined to a mental hospital after plunging into the abyss. ■ B.J.'s last days in Korea. ■ Father Mulcahy prays for the safety of his charges. ■ The traumatic death of a Korean woman's baby that pushed Hawkeye over the edge. ■ Klinger marries a young Korean woman and, ironically, stays in the country when the others leave. ■ Hot Lips and the arrogant Dr. Winchester.

after 10 seasons, but Twentieth Century Fox and CBS offered a shortened 11th season and an opportunity to "say goodbye" in an ambitious grand finale.

Titled "Goodbye, Farewell, and Amen," the two-and-a-half-hour final episode of *M*A*S*H*, which aired on February 28, 1983, became a national event and a linchpin of television history. Few sitcoms would have dared a movie-length finale, especially one heavy with tension and tragedy. Shot like a feature film, the show begins with a story involving Hawkeye based on real events that Metcalfe had gleaned from one of his interviews. The scene opens in a mental hospital, behind the closed doors of Ward D, where Hawkeye, who was always close to the edge, had finally plunged into the abyss. Beneath a ceiling fan, cast in shadow, and viewed from an awkward angle, he sits. Over several scenes viewers learn of a bus ride back from the beach gone horribly awry. Finally, Hawkeye, who has been repressing traumatic details, recalls that they were in danger of being overrun by a North Korean patrol, requiring everyone onboard to sit

(Jamie Farr), who'd spent the majority of his hitch wearing dresses in hopes of a Section 8 discharge. "I discovered that there were a number of men who had elected, once their tours of duty were over, to stay in Korea for whatever reason," explained Metcalfe. "Then we got to thinking, who would be the character whose staying in Korea would present the biggest surprise? Of course, it was Klinger, who had spent his entire career trying desperately to leave. So we evolved that story where he fell in love with a young Korean woman and ultimately married her and stayed there because of her."

It was the farewells that reduced much of the nation to tears. The close-knit cast's heartfelt emotion seemed genuine

yet avoided being sentimental. Alda later wrote that during the banquet scene the actors often "would sink into reveries" and were hungry for laughter—"we couldn't get enough of it."

Finally came Hawkeye and B.J.'s poignant final scene. Hawkeye had mocked B.J.'s inability to say goodbye, to accept that, living on opposite coasts, they'd most likely never see each other again. Both men struggle for words before their last embrace. Then B.J. rides out on a motorcycle and Hawkeye lifts off in a helicopter, smiling tearfully at the final note from his soul mate: On the ground, spelled out in white rocks, is the word "goodbye."

The buildup to the airing of the finale was unparalleled, weeks of media coverage that prompted *Washington Post* critic Tom Shales to complain, "The published anguish over

M*A*S*H's passing has reached a histrionic stage that is just short of embarrassing." To maintain suspense, CBS refused to let reviewers see advance copies.

The payoff was worthy of the hype. Critics hailed "Goodbye, Farewell, and Amen" as a masterpiece, a classic mix of the show's sharp wit and pathos. By commercial measures it was a phenomenon too—30-second ads cost a then-record $450,000. The finale earned a 60.3 rating and a 77 share, meaning 77 percent of the people watching television that night, at that time, were watching the finale. One newspaper calculated that Hawkeye and Margaret's farewell kiss lasted 34.8 seconds and thus was a $522,000 kiss.

> "The published anguish over *M*A*S*H*'s passing has reached a histrionic stage that is just short of embarrassing."

Another reported that New York City's water-flow rate jumped by 300 million gallons just after the show ended—in other words, an unheard-of number of people had been holding in trips to the bathroom until the credits rolled.

M*A*S*H remains a superstar of reruns, but the finale, watched by so many in 1983, is now rarely seen, since the world of syndication can't neatly accommodate it. Perhaps that is fitting—when the show does air, it remains a unique event, a reminder that, as creator Gelbart once said, "In the slum that television is, *M*A*S*H* looked like St. Paul's Cathedral."

Left to right: Hawkeye and Hot Lips say goodbye. ■ Colonel Potter's last ride. ■ B.J. and Hawkeye stumble through an awkward goodbye. ■ B.J.'s final message.

Cheers

"I'll Be Seeing You"

May 10, 1984

For its millions of faithful TV patrons, *Cheers* was a favorite Thursday night hangout for most of its 11 years on NBC. Sam, Diane, "Coach," Carla, Norm, Cliff, Woody, Rebecca, and all the colorful regulars at *Cheers* became as familiar as family, which is why *Cheers* was one of the longest running, most beloved television series of all time.

Cheers was the invention of the brother writing team Glen and Les Charles, and writer-director James Burrows. The Charles brothers got their start in 1974 after writing an episode for the legendary TV series *M*A*S*H*, a show that drew its strength from a powerful ensemble cast. Grant Tinker, head of MTM Productions, took notice and hired the duo as staff writers. Among other

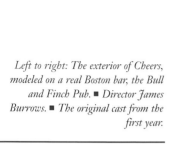

Left to right: The exterior of Cheers, modeled on a real Boston bar, the Bull and Finch Pub. ▪ Director James Burrows. ▪ The original cast from the first year.

shows, the two wrote for *The Bob Newhart Show* and *The Mary Tyler Moore Show*, again programs with talented ensembles. Eventually they were made producers on the *Mary Tyler Moore* spin-off *Phyllis*. From there they moved to Paramount TV and became producers and head writers on another classic show that featured a collection of off-the-wall characters, *Taxi*. That's where they hooked up with *Taxi*'s cocreator and director James Burrows. The trio stayed with *Taxi* for four years, and it brought them success and acclaim.

But the three men really wanted to work on a series of their own creation. So they left *Taxi* to form Charles Burrows Charles Productions. In a *TV Guide* interview, Glen Charles said, "We wanted to do an ensemble show like *M*A*S*H* or *Taxi*." Since all three were big fans of John Cleese's British comedy *Fawlty Towers*, they decided on a hotel as the setting for their new series. But after laying out the framework of their show, they realized that most of the scenes took place in the hotel's bar. That's when they opted to base the show in the bar itself, providing a setting in which an endless supply of characters could wander in and out. "It's much easier to write when you put all your characters in one room," Les Charles noted.

The only problem was how to avoid the seamy atmosphere usually associated with bars. They wanted something a little classier. So they based the *Cheers* bar on an actual Boston bar they were familiar with called the Bull and Finch Pub and, to avoid glorifying drinking, they made the owner of the bar a recovering alcoholic. Charles Burrows Charles then cast a group of relative unknowns, many of whom had guest-starred on *Taxi*.

Ted Danson starred as ex–Red Sox pitcher Sam "Mayday" Malone—the commitment-phobic, oversexed bar owner, who saw himself as God's irresistible gift to women. Irresistible, that is, to everyone except the reluctant, erudite barmaid Diane Chambers, played by Shelley Long. "We wanted to create a Katharine Hepburn/ Spencer Tracy type relationship," Burrows told the *New York Times*. Over the course of the series, Sam and Diane's on-again, off-again love-hate affair would provide some of the

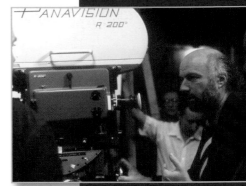

show's most affecting, and funniest, moments. "I had no glimmering of how to play the character whatsoever," Danson later revealed in an interview for *Entertainment Weekly*. "Here was a guy who was an alcoholic relief pitcher. Do you know the kind of arrogance that takes? I don't think I had the requisite disrespect you need to play this part until about the third or fourth year."

Cheers also made stars of its two philosophizing barflies, beer-loving, sometimes-employed accountant Norm Peterson, played by George Wendt, and Norm's best friend, know-it-all postman Cliff Clavin, played by John Ratzenberger. Ratzenberger described their role this way: "In classic drama you had the Greek chorus, the people that stood off to the side and commented on what was happening onstage. They would be the connection to the audience. So George and I referred to each other as the 'geek chorus.' We were the ones commenting on life."

Also in the mix were Rhea Perlman as acid-tongued waitress Carla Tortelli LeBec, and Nicholas Colasanto as dizzy ex–baseball coach Ernie Pantusso. The character of Dr. Frasier Crane, a stuffy, neurotic psychiatrist played by Kelsey Grammer, joined the show in 1984, and after Colasanto passed away in 1985, he was replaced by Woody Harrelson as the equally ditzy Woody Boyd. When Shelley Long left in 1987, Kirstie Alley, as the beautiful but tough Rebecca Howe, took her spot as Sam's foil.

Cheers debuted on NBC on September 30, 1982, to little acclaim. In fact, it was the lowest rated television show that week. And it didn't improve much that first season— finishing the year in 77th place. *Cheers* was almost canceled, but Grant Tinker, president of NBC, loved the show and

Left to right: Sam and Diane's love-hate relationship is philosophically observed by bar flies Norm and Cliff and scathingly denounced by acid-tongued waitress Carla. ■ Eventually, new characters joined the cast, replacing some of the regulars. ■ At the end of the second season, the on-again, off-again affair is finally ended when the couple stages a hilarious physical battle that signals the end of the relationship.

gave it another chance. Over the next year, as America came to love the *Cheers* family and the bar where "everybody knows your name," the show caught on and eventually became a huge hit with a devoted audience. It turned that cast of unknowns into household names, and one of the best TV ensembles ever.

Ratzenberger gives a lot of credit for the show's success to the writing. "And I think in large part, it had to do with how the writers of our show grew up reading books, not watching television," he says. "It made a big difference in the writing and the way the characters were developed. They weren't old story lines that you've already seen on old TV shows. It's really remarkable."

One of *Cheers*'s more memorable episodes was the year-ender for the second season, the second half of a two-parter titled "I'll Be Seeing You" that aired on May 10, 1984. In the first half, Sam is interviewed as one of Boston's "10 Most Eligible Bachelors," which makes Diane, who is "going with" Sam, furious. To make it up to her, Sam, on Cliff's advice, hires famed artist Phillip Semenko, played by Christopher Lloyd, to paint her portrait. Sam and the artist take an instant dislike to one another, and Sam ends up forbidding Diane to let Semenko paint her. This set the stage for Part 2, which ended the season with a "lust and anger" showdown between the star-crossed lovers.

Diane, of course, goes behind Sam's back and has her portrait—a study of her "tortured soul"—done. When she shows up at the bar with the finished painting, Sam is livid that she'd "disobeyed" him. The two get into a war of words—and then things get physical. In a closing scene that is at once hilariously funny, touching, and ultimately sad, the two take their love-hate relationship to the max. There's slapping and nose pinching, recriminations, and an ultimatum by Diane from which neither Sam nor Diane can back down. "It was in the timing of the slaps," Ratzenberger explains. "They could have slapped each other a lot of different ways, but it became funny and poignant because of the timing. . . . Somehow, without anyone saying it, you knew that this was a special moment, a moment that was going to last."

As Diane says, "This is it. We have sunk as low as human beings can sink!" the relationship is officially ended. When the show returned the following season, Diane came back with a new boyfriend, Dr. Frasier Crane.

Cheers ran for 11 seasons until, in 1992, Ted Danson, who at the time was making more than any other actor on series TV ($450,000 per episode) decided it was time to call it quits. In the series finale, for which the Charles brothers returned to the writing table, Sam and Diane have one last shot at marriage—and still can't cross the threshold.

The *Cheers* finale, its 275th episode, aired on May 20, 1993, and it received the second-best Nielsen rating of all time for an episodic TV program (trailing only *M*A*S*H*)—a 45.5 rating with a 64 audience share, which translated to 42,360,500 viewers.

In that show's poignant final scene, Sam Malone turns off the lights of his much-loved bar and locks the door as a mystery man walks down the steps toward the entrance and knocks on the window. When Sam utters the simple phrase "We're closed," 11 years of *Cheers* came to an end.

Cheers

The Tonight Show Starring Johnny Carson

"Funny Moments and a Final Farewell"

May 22, 1992

Right: Ed McMahon was Carson's side-kick from the beginning in 1962 until the last show. ■ *Bandleader Doc Severinsen played trumpet and straight man for Carson's wisecracks.* ■ *Events like the wacky wedding of strummer Tiny Tim and Miss Vicki were classic moments of Carson comedy.*

For Johnny Carson and his audience, it was a final trip down memory lane, filled with images and classic clips, each evoking a wave of laughter, a quiet tear, a flood of memories. Ed Ames's unforgettable tomahawk throw, an innocent demonstration turned indecent as the hatchet landed in the crotch of the stenciled target. The bizarre nuptials of show business oddity Tiny Tim and Miss Vicki. There was Johnny's mischievous proposition to Dolly Parton, offering her a year of his salary in exchange for a peek under her blouse. There were enough animals to fill the ark: talking birds that did or didn't speak, attacking leopards, snakes slithering up his pant leg, spiders crawling up his arm, and other sundry creatures relieving themselves on his desk or, worse, on him. Or any number of wonderful moments with Jack Benny, Jimmy Stewart, Angie Dickinson, Bob Hope, Jane Fonda, Don Rickles, Bob Newhart, Dyan Cannon, Sammy Davis Jr., and Burt Reynolds. Thirty years of memories in an hour, and then it was over. "And so it has come to this," Johnny Carson said as he sat pensively on a stool at center stage in front of his trademark Technicolor curtains, yet with the ubiquitous glint in his eyes. "I'm one of the lucky people in the world," he continued proudly. "I found something I always wanted to do, and I have enjoyed every single minute of it."

Those "minutes" turned into decades, marked by over 5,500 shows and nearly 24,000 guests. Carson's farewell *Tonight Show*, on May 22, 1992, was done his way. Just as the show had been done his way since he took over for Jack Paar 30 years before.

In 1962 Carson, 36, was already a television veteran with roots in the medium's earliest days. He made his television debut in Omaha, Nebraska, in 1949, hosting *The Squirrel's Nest*, an afternoon variety show. He moved to

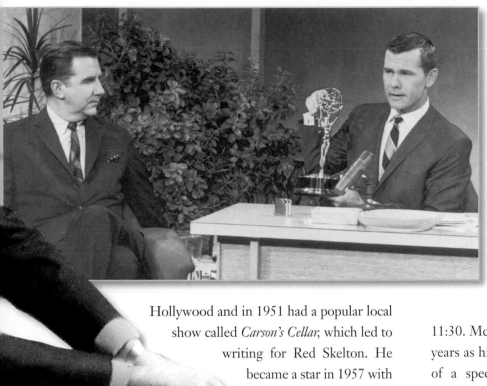

host, but Allen stayed less than two and a half years. The network used fill-ins like Ernie Kovacs for six months before hiring the mercurial Jack Paar. When Paar suddenly stepped down in 1962, the network turned to Carson, whose cool demeanor was the antithesis of his predecessor.

Carson, with McMahon at his side, took over October 1, and he changed not only the tone but the rules of *The Tonight Show*. He refused to deliver his monologue—the linchpin of his show—at 11:15, before many affiliates were tuned in, so NBC started the show at

Hollywood and in 1951 had a popular local show called *Carson's Cellar*, which led to writing for Red Skelton. He became a star in 1957 with the ABC game show *Who Do You Trust?* which he hosted for five years. His sidekick on that show was an announcer from Philadelphia named Ed McMahon.

Meanwhile, NBC's *Tonight Show* had become a hit but an unstable one. It debuted in 1954 with Steve Allen as

11:30. McMahon remembers the first seven years as his favorite era. "That is really kind of a special time, when you're creating something," he says.

In May 1972, Carson moved the show from New York to Burbank. He insisted on cutting his workweek to four days, by scheduling repeats and fill-in guest hosts like Jay Leno and Joan Rivers on Mondays, and ultimately reducing the show from 90

The Tonight Show Starring Johnny Carson

minutes to an hour. He also formed Carson Productions, taking ownership of the show, so he would have complete control.

But he could never have gained such clout backstage without attaining unparalleled success in front of the camera. Carson's comedic timing was impeccable; he had an expressive face and the ideal humor for Americans getting ready for bed. His monologue became America's bedtime story. His characters, from smart-aleck psychic Carnac the Magnificent to salacious *Tea Time Movie* host Art Fern to the lovable old Aunt Blabby, became beloved classics.

Carson's comedic timing was impeccable; he had an expressive face and the ideal humor for Americans getting ready for bed.

And while celebrities and musicians were staples, Carson was always at his best with animals and eccentrics. "He loved real people and he loved the animals," McMahon remembers. "And he knew that he could milk that stuff, you know; he knew how to make it work. You know, 'The mynah bird will say 47 words, okay.' Here's the mynah bird. And the mynah bird says nothing. Well, the look on his face, the asides to me. It was pure joy for him. He loved that."

On October 16, 1987, one such unconventional guest, Myrtle Young, appeared on the show with her potato chip collection, showing off chips that looked like an "angry dog," "a sleeping bird," and Yogi Bear. When McMahon

distracted Young momentarily, Carson popped into his mouth an ordinary chip he had hidden behind his desk. The loud crunch produced a look of shock, bewilderment and, finally, relief on Young's face. "That moment, like so many great Carson moments, was unrehearsed," says McMahon. "I wasn't in on the gag," he recalls, adding that Carson just took advantage of the moment. "I thought she was going to keel over. I really did."

Behind the scenes, however, life was much more routine. Carson would start writing jokes in the margins of his morning newspaper at home in Malibu. Both McMahon and Carson would arrive at the studio in the afternoon, but their paths wouldn't cross until 4:30—an hour before taping—in the makeup room. McMahon says that at about 5:15 he'd spend five to 10 minutes visiting with Carson, discussing anything and everything . . . except the show. "It could be something in a political sense or religious—whatever was happening. He thinks funny, and it always became funny," McMahon recalls. Then McMahon and Carson had one final ritual. About seven minutes before show time, "I'd shake his hand and say, 'I'll see you up there,'" McMahon recalls. And then it was "Here's Johnny . . ."

1982

Left to right: Johnny made the most of animal antics and weird personalities like Art Fern, Carnac the Magnificent, and Aunt Blabby.

By the 1990s television was shifting, and NBC had two potential heirs, Leno and David Letterman, waiting impatiently in the wings. Whether Carson was given a shove (as was widely rumored) or he simply decided to go out on top, he announced in 1991 that he'd abdicate his throne at the 30-year mark.

In the final weeks the ovations before Carson's monologue kept growing louder and longer. For his last regular show, the applause lasted two minutes and 15 seconds, embarrassing the host. The show featured a typically manic Robin Williams and diva Bette Midler, who serenaded Carson and even coerced him into a duet of "Here's That Rainy Day," one of his favorite songs. "That was one of the most inspired and one of the most beautifully performed shows of all times of the regular genre of the show," McMahon insists. It was so rousing, so perfect, that in postproduction Carson briefly mused that it would be difficult to top, and that maybe they should cancel the finale.

NBC gave Carson free range for the finale, offering him a prime-time slot, saying he could take three hours, do it live, do, essentially, whatever he wanted. "The last show had to be different, and Johnny was smart enough to know that," McMahon says.

Carson was uncomfortable with a self-serving, celebrity-studded prime-time extravaganza. He wanted the equivalent of sitting on a porch and reminiscing before saying good-bye. It was Carson's idea to sit on the stool and introduce favorite clips, his idea to have only family and friends of the staff in the audience, his idea to write the monologue himself. In fact, no one on the show knew exactly what he was going to say before he went on camera.

He was more soft-spoken, more sentimental and reflective than usual, telling the 50 million viewers, "I cannot imagine finding something in television after I leave tonight that would give me as much joy and pleasure, and such a sense of exhilaration, as this show has given me. It's just hard to explain." But he also kept joking till the end, and his jokes were vintage Carson: "I am taking the applause sign home—putting it in the bedroom. And maybe once a week—just turn it on."

The show ended with Carson, flanked by McMahon and flamboyant bandleader Doc Severinsen, addressing the audience directly. "You people watching, I can only tell you it has been an honor and a privilege to come into your homes all these years and entertain you. And I hope when I find something I want to do and I think you will like, that you'll be as gracious in inviting me into you home as you have been. I bid you a very heartfelt good night." Carson blew a kiss to the audience and walked off the set, his image dissolving to a photograph of a sunset taken by his son Rick shortly before his tragic death in a 1991 auto accident, as the credits rolled.

Left to right: In 1991, with rivals David Letterman and Jay Leno waiting in the wings, Carson decided to give up his throne after 30 years. ■ The final show featured special guests Robin Williams and Bette Midler. ■ It was Carson's own idea to sit on a stool and introduce his favorite clips from the show's history, and he was moved to tears by the sentimental moments of the last monologue.

Afterward Carson left by helicopter while the staff snatched up mementos from the studio. That night he hosted a lavish party at his house—there were no NBC executives and no celebrities, however, just his staff and their families, enjoying a final, private thank-you.

"I admired him," McMahon proclaims. "I thought he was the best thing that ever happened to television."

As late night fragmented, with Letterman, Leno, Conan O'Brien, Craig Kilborn, and others carving up the landscape, it became clear that Carson's timing had again been perfect—television had changed forever, and there would be only one king of late night: Johnny Carson.

The Tonight Show Starring Johnny Carson

Survivor
Season One

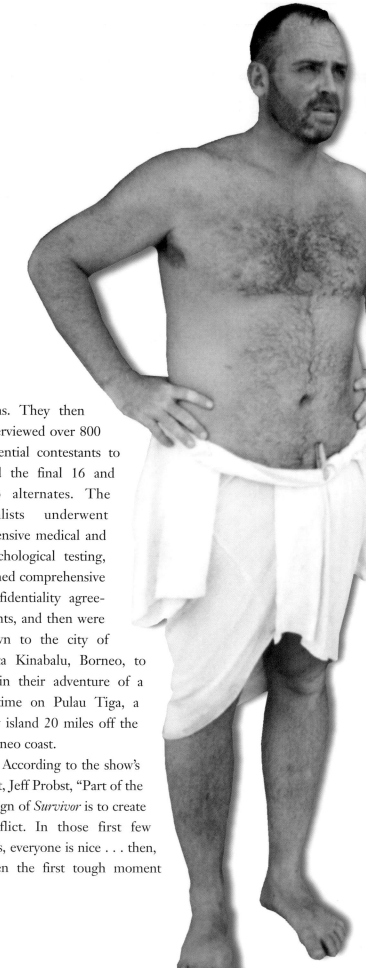

August 24, 2000

Right: The Pulau Tiga island group from the first season. ■ *Grimaces punctuate the challenge of swallowing bugs and grubs, but the bared tongue signals victory.*

Sixteen strangers on an Indonesian sailing schooner in the middle of the South China Sea were suddenly given just two minutes to grab whatever provisions they could, cut loose two rafts, jump ship, and paddle four hours to a secluded island where they would live for the next 39 days. "Forced to band together . . . learn to adapt or be voted off. In the end, one will leave the island with a million dollars in cash as their reward. Thirty-nine days—16 people—one Survivor!" And so began one of the first and most successful of a genre of prime-time programs dubbed "reality TV," born out of fear, first of a writers' strike, then of an actors' strike, that gripped the television networks in 2000.

The idea was simple. Isolate 16 ordinary people and, under the ever-present eye of the camera, watch as they scheme and struggle to "Outwit, Outplay, and Outlast" one another under some of the most "unreal" of circumstances.

Survivor was the brainchild of British television producer Charlie Parsons, who developed the series with fellow producer and former British Army Special Services member Mark Burnett. With that milion-dollar enticement, Parsons and Burnett were deluged with 6,000 videotaped applica-

tions. They then interviewed over 800 potential contestants to find the final 16 and two alternates. The finalists underwent extensive medical and psychological testing, signed comprehensive confidentiality agreements, and then were flown to the city of Kota Kinabalu, Borneo, to begin their adventure of a lifetime on Pulau Tiga, a tiny island 20 miles off the Borneo coast.

According to the show's host, Jeff Probst, "Part of the design of *Survivor* is to create conflict. In those first few days, everyone is nice . . . then, when the first tough moment hits, that first night in the rain, or the first day without food . . . [it] starts to build inside you. All of a sudden, the truth comes out."

Divided into two "tribes," Tagi and Pagong, named for their respective beach locations, the castaways were deprived of the comforts of civilization, then made to compete in "challenges," diabolical tests of physical and mental stamina ranging from elaborate obstacle courses to grueling competitions of will and endurance.

One was a "reward challenge," in which castaways competed for prizes such as telephone privileges or a hot shower. The second was an "immunity challenge," in which they competed for immunity from being voted off the island. The winning team of an immunity challenge did not have to vote a member off at the end of the episode. "The real purpose behind the challenge," according to Probst, "is to create more reality. So the challenges are usually built so that you have to pick a leader or you have to leave someone behind or in a situation where they're going to have to fight to stay alive. They're just another way to instigate more conflict."

That first season, almost everyone in the *Survivor* crew was involved in testing the challenges—and that included eating the thumb-size grubs that were the centerpiece of one of the show's most memorable and cringe-inducing challenges. "If you were on a deserted island, what would you do, starve or eat this? That was the original purpose behind having a food challenge," says Probst. "If everybody else has eaten and it comes down to you and that other guy, and he's eating it, are you going to eat it or are you going to sit there and say, 'Guys, I'm sorry, I just can't do it'? That's the challenge that made that interesting." To their surprise, the testing led to an unexpected problem for the producers—crew members actually developed an appetite for the creatures. "We got into bug eating, quite frankly," Burnett recalls. "We had a number of Malaysians . . . on the crew, and they loved eating them. It's a delicacy there. The whole challenge crew got into it. . . . I thought they were

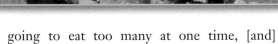

going to eat too many at one time, [and] there'd be none left."

Another of the challenges provided a more serious problem for the producers—one that could have shut down the show. Contestant Richard Hatch persuaded the remaining survivors to mutiny. "We were down to five people, and Hatch convinced them that the reward [for that particular challenge] was going to be simply a cold beer," remembers Jeff Probst. "And that . . . wasn't enough." Hatch persuaded the rest that there was nothing the producers could do to make them undertake that challenge. "So they're walking toward us," Probst continued, "and the producers radio and say, 'Guys, we have a mutiny.' This happens to be the one day that all the sponsors have flown in from the United States. And we're telling [the sponsors], 'Uh, it's going great, you're not going to believe it.'"

Quick thinking by Burnett and his crew headed off a disaster. They upped the stakes—the winner of the challenge would get the cold

beer, but also a hot dinner and a chance to see a tape of himself or herself in the first 10 minutes of Episode One. That did it. "Richard shows up, very smug, ready to pounce on me," says Probst. "And then I laid out the rest of it, and the other four turned on him like, 'You don't know what you're talking about.' And we were saved."

Alliances among tribal members were formed and re-formed, then re-formed again depending the outcomes of the various challenges. Every three days tribe members participated in the Tribal Council ceremony. There, members were allowed to vent and vote another one of their own off the island. The ritual ended with the torch of the ousted member being snuffed out, symbolizing banishment, as Probst solemnly proclaimed, "The tribe has spoken."

Though early eliminations were to a large extent based on castaways' physical deficiencies, in the later rounds, it was the ability to outthink that kept people on the island. Perhaps the finale's, and the whole first year's, most dramatic moment came during Wisconsin truck driver Susan Hawk's rancorous speech at the final Tribal Council. At one point in the game, Hawk had allied herself with Las Vegas river guide Kelly Wiglesworth, only to find that she'd been duped. Still fuming from the betrayal, Hawk unflatteringly compared eventual winner Richard Hatch to a snake and Wiglesworth to a rat. And, to Hawk's way of thinking, a "snake" like Hatch, who'd never lied about his manipulations, was more deserving than the "rat" who'd lied to her. In casting her vote for Hatch, Hawk declared, "Mother Nature intended it to be, for the snake to eat the rat."

Richard Hatch, a 39-year-old, gay former soldier and corporate communications consultant from Rhode Island, became *Survivor*'s first million-dollar winner. The key to winning *Survivor* was, according to Probst, "Adaptability. Richard was very good at assessing the situation from

Left to right: Americans were glued to their television sets as the teams chopped bamboo for shelter and exercised survival techniques to stay competitive. ■ *Host Jeff Probst snuffs a losing contestant's torch.* ■ *Wiglesworth and Hatch plead their cases during the final tribal council vote.* ■ *Probst displays a vote against Hatch.* ■ *Hatch reacts on learning that he is the winner of the million-dollar prize.*

moment to moment. He went out and he started catching fish. And became the food provider. And he didn't ever forget to remind people, 'I caught that fish. I just want to remind you that you're eating because of me. So keep me around.' He was a master at manipulating those guys."

Over 125 million viewers watched all or part of the inaugural season, and a staggering 51 million people watched the finale, making it the second biggest TV show of 2000, behind only Super Bowl XXXIV. The television tribe had spoken, making *Survivor* a genuine cultural phenomenon.

Alliances among tribal members were formed and re-formed, then re-formed again depending the outcomes of the various challenges.

Unforgettable Moments in Television **News**

Nixon's Checkers Speech

September 23, 1952

Richard Nixon once wrote, "Of all institutions arrayed against a president, none controls his fate more than television." No national politician of the television age seemed to know that better yet, at the same time, appear to understand it less, than Richard Nixon.

By the summer of 1952, 39-year-old California freshman senator Richard Nixon was already among the most famous—and controversial—politicians of his day. As a member of the House Un-American Activities Committee, his aggressive investigation of former State Department official Alger Hiss made him a hero to the right wing of the Republican Party. In six short years he'd gone from an obscure California congressman to the vice presidential running mate of popular World War II hero Dwight D. Eisenhower.

But halfway through the campaign, Nixon was almost dropped from the ticket. A group of wealthy businessmen from California had raised $18,000 for

Left top: In 1952 Nixon was almost dropped from the ticket as Eisenhower's running mate. Bottom: The front page of the New York Post *alleging that Nixon donors expected to receive special favors. Right: Nixon and former New York governor Thomas Dewey.*

Nixon's run. Political reporters from the *New York Post* uncovered the story and alleged that the donors expected to receive "special favors" from Nixon when he became vice president. The headline in the newspaper read SECRET RICH MEN'S TRUST FUND KEEPS NIXON IN STYLE FAR BEYOND HIS SALARY. It was the first shot in what became known as the "Fund Crisis," and Eisenhower was furious. In his run for the presidency, Eisenhower had been critical of corruption in the Truman administration, and he believed the taint of a scandal on his own team could undermine his whole campaign.

It is said that Eisenhower intimated through aides that it would be a good thing if Nixon resigned gracefully from the ticket. Nixon waited to speak with Eisenhower himself. His ally Murray Chotiner suggested that Nixon use the money that was allocated for a vice presidential TV program to answer the charges. Former New York governor Thomas Dewey, another of Nixon's supporters, concurred. "Eisenhower's advisers are a hanging jury. I think what you ought to do is to go on TV and ask the people to indicate whether they support you or not."

Nixon finally got the call from Eisenhower himself, and the two discussed the strategy of answering the charges on television. Eisenhower was for it, and instructed Nixon to not only answer the allegations but also, "Tell the country everything you have ever received, how much money you have earned, what it's been used for, what your worth is."

"Well, General," said Nixon, "I'll be glad to do that because I've got nothing to hide."

Nixon took his case to the American people. That plea, which came to be known as the "Checkers" or "Republican Cloth Coat" speech, was televised on September 23, 1952. The show was broadcast from a studio in the El Capitan Theatre in Hollywood. Nixon sat at a desk, and his wife, Pat, sat beside him. Throughout the speech, Nixon projected humility and credibility. Beginning his plea with the now-familiar phrase "My Fellow Americans," Nixon proved himself as both a viable candidate and a compelling speaker. "I come before you tonight as a candidate for the vice presidency," he began, "and as a man whose honesty and integrity have been questioned." Continuing, he sought to distinguish himself as a man of honor and simultaneously attack sitting president Harry S. Truman. "Now, the usual thing to do when charges are made against you is to either ignore them or deny them without giving details. I believe we have had enough of that in the United States, particularly with the present administration in Washington, D.C."

Then he laid out the case against him. "I am sure that you have read the charges, and you have heard it, that I, Senator Nixon, took $18,000 from a group of my supporters." And he proceeded methodically to lay himself bare

before the American people, not only countering the charges but cementing himself in the national consciousness as "just plain folks" with phrases like "I don't happen to be a rich man." He presented his family's history, includ-

> "The decision, my friends, is not mine. . . . I am submitting to the Republican National Committee tonight the decision which it is theirs to make."

ing his father's grocery store and his experiences working his way through law school. He even presented his own family finances in detail: his $4,000 life insurance policy, their 1950 Oldsmobile, and their $13,000 home in Whittier, California, on which they still owed $10,000.

To most politicians, these revelations would have been too great to air. But Richard Nixon had a couple of more bathetic arrows in his quiver—two more shots at endearing himself to the "common folk."

"Well, that's about it," he summed up. "That's what we have and that's what we owe. It isn't very much, but Pat and I have the satisfaction that every dime that we've got is honestly ours. I should say this—that Pat doesn't have a mink coat. But she does have a respectable Republican cloth coat."

Then, for what became the centerpiece of the historic speech, Nixon borrowed a shrewd tactic from former president Franklin Roosevelt. "I always admired FDR as a great politician," Nixon said in a 1983 interview. "He really decimated his opponents in one of his campaigns when he was answering some of the attacks and said these attacks were unfair against him. Then he went on to say, 'And I suppose next they're going to be attacking my dog Fala.' So that's why I said what I did about Checkers."

"One other thing I probably should tell you. . . . We did get something—a gift—after the election. A man down in Texas heard Pat on the radio mention the fact that our two youngsters would like to have a dog. . . . We got a message from the Union Station in Baltimore saying they had a package for us. . . . You know what it was? It was a little cocker spaniel in a crate. . . . Black and white, spotted. And our little girl, Tricia, the six-year-old, named it Checkers. And you know, the kids love that dog and I just want to say

this right now, that regardless of what they say about it, we're going to keep it."

"There were a lot of people in Texas, incidentally, that liked the fact that that dog came from Texas," Nixon said in later years. "And we carried Texas, finally."

It was reported at the time that the "Checkers" part of the speech actually had viewers crying. Then Nixon took the burden off his own shoulders. "The decision, my friends, is not mine. . . ." he said. "I am submitting to the Republican National Committee tonight the decision which it is theirs to make." But then the wily senator took the decision away from the Republican Party and put it squarely on the shoulders of the American people. "And I am going to ask you to help them decide. Wire and write the Republican National Committee whether you think I should stay on or whether I should get off. And whatever their decision is, I will abide by it."

The Checkers speech was incredibly effective. It lasted 30 minutes and brought Nixon, who had been in the Senate for only a year and a half, unprecedented publicity. The nation was definitely interested. The broadcast was seen by the largest television audience ever to watch a political program to date—60 million were tuned in, fully half the sets in the U.S.

Ironically, Nixon initially believed the speech was a

failure. He had missed the cue to tell the viewers where to send their wires. Instead, they were sent to Eisenhower, to the hotel where the Nixons were staying, to their home in California, to his office in Washington, and to the Republican National Committee. When Nixon arrived back at his hotel the first call he received was from movie producer Daryl Zanuck. According to Nixon, Zanuck delivered a rave review. "There's never been political television like that," he said. "There'll never be any like that again."

In the following days, the campaign was flooded with an unbelievable three million letters and two million telegrams, and Richard M. Nixon kept his spot on the 1952 Republican ticket. In November, Ike and Dick trounced Adlai E. Stevenson and John Sparkman, and in January, they assumed the offices of president and vice president.

This was perhaps Nixon's finest hour on television; the telecast saved his political career. But the medium of television would not serve Nixon well in the following years. In the case of the nationally televised debates versus John F. Kennedy in 1960, his dark physical demeanor would counter his political savvy and possibly cost him that year's presidential election.

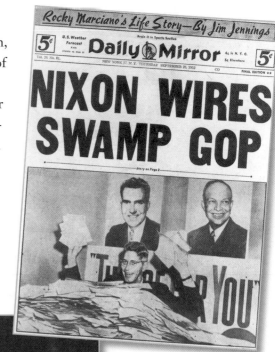

Left to right: Nixon and his wife, Pat, prepare for his address to the nation over radio and television. ■ The successful speech projected an image of earnest integrity that appealed to the American public. ■ As reported in New York's Daily Mirror, *the public rallied in support of Nixon, and Eisenhower kept him as the Republican candidate for vice president.*

The First Great Debate

Kennedy versus Nixon

Left to right: Kennedy and Nixon were the first presidential candidates to stage a formal televised debate. ▪ CBS News producer Don Hewitt briefs Kennedy and his communications adviser, J. Leonard Reinsch.

September 26, 1960

On September 26, 1960, at CBS station WBBM in Chicago, the Republican nominee, Vice President Richard Nixon, debated his rival for the presidency, Democratic Senator John F. Kennedy. It was the first debate of its kind to be broadcast on national television, and while little is remembered of what was actually said that night, the results were weighty enough to affect the outcome of that year's election and the way America would select its presidents for years to come.

The first debate consisted mostly of two skilled campaigners offering well-rehearsed political axioms like "I think it's time America started moving again" and "When you're in a race, the only way to stay ahead is to move ahead." Yet the country was riveted by the spectacle of presidential campaigners squaring off before millions looking on from their living rooms. For Kennedy, still largely unknown, the debates were a calling card, and his best opportunity to convince skeptics that he possessed the maturity and experience the presidency requires. For Nixon, a familiar face after eight years as vice president, the debates were an equally crucial opportunity to reinforce the common wisdom that maturity and experience were his strong suits.

With few serious differences of policy separating the candidates, the debates were all but certain to turn on matters of presentation and style, a point Kennedy tried to use to his advantage. A week before the first debate, he interrupted his campaign to meet with the director-producer of the debates, Don Hewitt of CBS News (later of *60 Minutes* fame), peppering him with questions about logistics and camera shots. "We met in a hangar at Midway Airport in Chicago," recalls Hewitt. "Kennedy was very curious. He wanted to know, 'Where do I stand?' 'How long do I have to answer?' 'Will I get a warning when I've gone too far?' He really wanted to know the nuts and bolts of what we were going to do."

Kennedy, who had been campaigning in California that week, spent the afternoon of the debate resting in his hotel. He showed up tanned and ready. Nixon, who had vowed to visit all 50 states before the election, was physically drained and looked it. He was also suffering from a staphylococcus infection, the result of having badly banged his knee the day before. But instead of resting up for the debate, he spent the day meeting with the local plumbers union. "I never saw Nixon before they arrived in the studio that night," recalls Hewitt. "Jack Kennedy knew that an election could ride on this television appearance. Nixon thought it was just another campaign stop."

Once the candidates were seated together, Kennedy and Nixon were offered makeup. Kennedy declined, so Nixon did as well, apparently wary of public reaction if word got out. However, Kennedy aide Ted

"My God, we just elected a president of the United States, and it isn't even election day."

Sorensen later told Hewitt that the Kennedy team had secretly applied a light coat of makeup to their candidate's face behind the closed doors of his dressing room. At the last minute, Nixon's advisers applied a product called Lazy Shave to lighten up his five o'clock shadow, but it didn't have much effect.

The color of Nixon's suit was also less than ideal. Its light tone nearly blended into the background, whereas Kennedy's darker suit provided a better contrast with the set. (The debates, like all television shows at the time, were broadcast in black and white). Hewitt felt concerned enough about the unfairness of the color difference that he approached CBS president Frank Stanton about it. Stanton then asked Nixon adviser Ted Rogers if he was satisfied with everything. When

Rogers said yes, Nixon looked fine to him, Stanton decided that offering any further advice would be interfering.

Periodically during the debate Hewitt employed a television technique called a reaction shot, showing one candidate's reaction to what the other was saying. Kennedy's reactions showed him to be attentive, confident, and occasionally amused, with a slight smile playing on his lips. Nixon seemed haggard, tense, and generally less self-assured. He could present a case for his greater maturity and experience, but he didn't look the part.

Consequently, while the majority of radio listeners thought that Nixon had fared better than Kennedy, the majority of the seventy million Americans who watched the debates on TV felt differently. They had witnessed a perspiring, weary-looking vice president trumped by a vigorous, virile-looking senator.

Hewitt says he recognized the impact of Kennedy's performance immediately. "As I left the control room that night I said to myself, 'My God, we just elected a president of the United States, and it isn't even election day.'"

The effect of the debate on Kennedy's campaign was

evident. The senator from Massachusetts was transformed into a national celebrity, and his appearances were greeted by surging throngs. "In hindsight Nixon must have said to himself, 'Why did I do that?' I mean, 'Why did I give this guy the exposure?'" Hewitt surmises. "Jack Kennedy making speeches is a bore. Jack Kennedy debating Richard Nixon is an event."

Nixon prepared better for the three subsequent debates, which were held on October 7, 13, and 21, 1960—and he wore makeup each time. But, as the saying goes, you never get a second chance to make a first impression. On election day a Roper survey found that 57 percent of the voters were influenced by the debates and 6 percent based their final decision on them. Kennedy was elected president by less than 1 percent of the vote, winning the popular tally by a margin of 118,550, and taking 303 electoral votes to Nixon's 219.

In retrospect, given Kennedy's painstakingly concealed health problems—the chronic back ailments and Addison's disease, which required frequent medication—his physically impressive showing in the first 1960 debate was ironic, underscoring the limitations of television as a guide to public decision making. After viewing a film of one of his TV appearances, Kennedy remarked, "We wouldn't have had a prayer without that gadget."

Four years later, at the 1964 Republican National Convention, Nixon was slated to introduce that year's presidential nominee, Barry Goldwater. Before delivering the speech, he had his makeup applied by Frances Arvold. Hewitt, who was present, told Nixon, "If you had let Frances do that four years ago, then Barry Goldwater would be introducing you." Hewitt recalls Nixon replying, "You know, you're probably right."

Nixon went on to win election as president in 1968 by a razor-thin margin over Vice President Hubert Humphrey, and he was reelected by a landslide over Senator George McGovern in 1972. There were no televised debates in either of those campaigns. The TV debate tradition returned to American politics in the 1976 campaign for president between Jimmy Carter and Gerald Ford—two years after Richard Nixon resigned from the presidency.

Four Days in November

Top left: President John F. Kennedy riding in the motorcade approximately one minute before he was shot. Far right: Walter Cronkite announces the death of President Kennedy.

November 22–25, 1963

Just as FDR used *radio* to rally a nation weary from depression and war, John F. Kennedy used *television* to empower his presidency. Throughout his campaign and his thousand days in office, Kennedy used the small screen to convey the vision of his "new frontier." He used it to underscore the importance of the civil rights struggle and to explain to the world the perilous no-win prospects of global nuclear warfare. But it was his fateful final day in office and the three that followed that would irreversibly fuse his legacy to television, and in the process elevate television to its position as the nation's primary source for news and information.

The four tumultuous days began innocently enough on the clear crisp morning of Friday, November 22, 1963. President John F. Kennedy and his wife, Jackie, flew from San Antonio

to Dallas where he was scheduled to give a luncheon speech at the Trade Mart building. At about 12:30 P.M. CST, as the presidential motorcade made its way from Love Field to

downtown Dallas, the open-air limousine traversed Dealey Plaza, near the Texas School Book Depository building. Suddenly, the triumphant spectacle turned tragic. The joyous cheering was replaced by screams of disbelief as the cracking sound of gunfire echoed between the buildings. Kennedy was hit twice. As the presidential party sped toward Parkland Memorial Hospital, the scene in downtown Dallas turned to panic, and the crowd began fleeing in every direction, running for safety.

The news of what had actually happened was sketchy at best. The view of the White House press corps traveling with Kennedy was obstructed due to its position at the tail end of the motorcade. Merriman Smith, the United Press International senior White House correspondent, hastily filed the first report. At approximately 12:34 P.M. CST, radio and television stations across the nation began hearing the startling clacking sound of their UPI teletype machines indicating a breaking news bulletin. It read simply: DALLAS, NOV. 22 (UPI) THREE SHOTS WERE FIRED AT PRESIDENT KENNEDY'S MOTORCADE IN DOWNTOWN DALLAS.

Within minutes, ABC Radio's Don Gardiner was on the network with the announcement. On CBS the popular soap opera *As the World Turns* was suddenly preempted by a voice-over bulletin from anchor Walter Cronkite repeating the UPI report. In 1963, the NBC television network was "down" at that time of day, allowing affiliates to air locally produced programming. By 1:53 P.M. EST, the NBC affiliates had rejoined the network, and Chet Huntley and Bill Ryan were anchoring.

For most of the next hour, the nation nervously awaited news of the president's condition, and watched as the three networks spoke by telephone to their correspondents in Dallas, desperate to separate reality from rumor. Footage of Kennedy's breakfast with the Fort Worth Chamber of Commerce filmed ear-

lier that morning was interspersed with reports from the hospital in Dallas. Shortly after two P.M. EST, the CBS radio network broke with the announcement that President Kennedy had died.

Despite the radio report, the policy of the CBS television news department was to wait for confirmation from a print source or wire service. (At the time, the electronic press was hesitant to report a story without first confirming it with a reliable print source.) Then at 2:38 P.M. EST, teary-eyed, his baritone cracking, Cronkite went on the air

to deliver the news that would leave an indelible image in the mind of everyone who watched it: "From Dallas, Texas, a flash, apparently official. President Kennedy died at one P.M., central standard time, two o'clock eastern standard time, some thirty-eight minutes ago." Cronkite's loss of composure was unusual for the seasoned reporter, prompting the head of CBS News, Sig Mickelson, to send him home. Newsman Charles Collingwood took over.

At that point in history, there were no "all-news" television networks. CBS and NBC had only recently expanded their nightly news shows from 15 minutes to one half hour.

But for the next four days, in an unprecedented move, the existing three networks, CBS, NBC, and ABC, canceled regular programming and commercials to cover the national tragedy. That weekend, as many as nine out of 10 Americans

"From Dallas, Texas, a flash, apparently official. President Kennedy died at one P.M., central standard time."

remained glued to their TV sets mourning and seeking answers. Indeed, for over 70 hours, television provided uninterrupted, noncommercial coverage of the events.

Throughout the weekend, disbelief ripped through the nation as television tracked two interlinked stories. The first involved the actual crime. Almost immediately, Dallas police suspected that Lee Harvey Oswald, who worked at the Texas School Book Depository, was the culprit. Their suspicions were heightened after a police officer was shot and killed; police tracked Oswald to a movie theater, where he was subdued and arrested on Friday afternoon.

Meanwhile, the networks followed a second, equally significant and compelling story: the preparations for President Kennedy's funeral, beginning with the transfer of the president's body to Washington, D.C. Television displayed images of his grieving widow, still wearing her blood-stained pink suit, as her husband's body arrived in Washington and

Left to right: President Lyndon Johnson makes his first statement after the assassination. ▪ A television news conference surrounds guards and secret service agents escorting Lee Harvey Oswald at Dallas police headquarters. ▪ Live television captures nightclub owner Jack Ruby as he approaches and shoots Oswald fatally in the stomach.

then was delivered to Bethesda Naval Hospital for the autopsy. And television showed the world that the transfer of power to the incoming president, Lyndon B. Johnson, had been peacefully achieved. Johnson, who had been sworn in on the plane, made a brief statement and concluded by saying, "I will do my best. That is all I can do. I ask for your help, and God's."

Via television, Americans got their first look at the suspect, who was taken to the Dallas city jail. Nearly a hundred reporters descended on the jail, lining the corridors and shouting questions as a manacled Oswald was shuttled in and out of interrogation. Bowing to demands from the assembled press corps, Dallas police held a hurried press conference after midnight on Friday, holding up the rifle and triumphantly proclaiming it the "murder weapon," and allowing journalists to fire questions at Oswald.

The scene in Dallas remained confused on Saturday while reporters delved into Oswald's personal life. As the

FBI and police continued to interrogate Oswald, it was announced that the accused assassin would be transferred from the city jail to the county lockup, thought to be a more secure facility and more accommodating for the ever-growing horde of news reporters. The Justice Department requested that the transfer take place secretly at night, but Dallas police chief Jess Curry scheduled the transfer for noon on Sunday. The media would be permitted to cover the transfer, and NBC Television opted to telecast the event live.

On Sunday afternoon, at approximately 12:20 P.M. EST, Kennedy's coffin was moved from the White House to the Capitol, borne on a horse-drawn caisson. After a speech by Senate Majority Leader Mike Mansfield, the Capitol rotunda was opened so the public could view the casket and pay their last respects. ABC and CBS broadcast the solemn ceremony.

At about that same time in Dallas, Oswald emerged from the basement of the jail, handcuffed and flanked by detectives, for the short walk to a waiting armored truck.

He never got there. As Oswald took his first steps down the hallway filled with reporters, millions watched in horror as Dallas nightclub owner Jack Ruby stepped forward and shot him in the stomach with a Colt .38 revolver. Standing just feet from Oswald, NBC reporter Tom Pettit, in an incredulous tone, began shouting, "He's been shot! Lee Harvey Oswald's been shot!"

saluting his father, a particularly poignant moment given that it was John-John's third birthday; and the Kennedy family taking its place behind the horse-drawn caisson for the long 45-minute walk to St. Matthews Cathedral.

The television audience then watched as the funeral motorcade left for Arlington National Cemetery. After a brief ceremony at the grave site, "Taps" was played. Then the eternal flame that stands watch over President Kennedy's grave was lit.

According to A. C. Nielsen audience research, the average home in their survey tuned in for a total of 31.6 hours that weekend. Monday, the day of the funeral, was the heaviest viewing day. Approximately 93 percent of television homes in the U.S. watched the funeral procession. Additionally, the funeral was telecast via satellite to 23 countries around the world and viewed by more than 600 million people.

Ruby was arrested. Oswald was taken to Parkland Memorial Hospital, where an hour later he was pronounced dead. The nation was shocked by the second assassination in two days.

The next day, President Kennedy was laid to rest at Arlington National Cemetery. It would take the combined efforts of the three television networks to allow the country to view the funeral and mourn collectively. While each network provided its own team of commentators, it was necessary that they combine their resources to establish the over 40 camera positions necessary to provide the unprecedented coverage. Those who watched will never forget the collage of flickering TV images: the riderless horse; the president's son, John Jr.,

With their wall-to-wall coverage, the CBS and NBC television networks each lost an estimated $4 million, and ABC lost approximately $2 million. But in doing so, television news entered adulthood. Coverage of the Kennedy assassination provided a template for future events. One observer wrote, "It was the event that legitimized television in the eyes of the public. . . . Print would never again challenge television as the public's primary source of information and authority." From the assassinations of Rev. Dr. Martin Luther King Jr. and Senator Robert Kennedy in 1968 to the *Challenger* explosion in

"It was the event that legitimized television in the eyes of the public."

1986 to the destruction of the World Trade Center towers on September 11, 2001, Americans turned to television for both information and solace.

As veteran television news producer Don Hewitt said, "If a plane is taken hostage or there's a baby in a well, the country goes to their televisions. And it started that day in Dallas."

Left to right: The caisson carrying Kennedy's casket leaves the White House for the Capitol. ■ *Honor guards, the Kennedy family, and government officials attend the memorial service in the Capitol Rotunda.* ■ *A French family gathers in front of the television, adorned with photos of Kennedy, to watch his funeral.* ■ *The funeral procession winds its way from St. Matthew's Cathedral to Arlington National Cemetery.* ■ *Three-year-old John F. Kennedy Jr. salutes his father's casket.*

Vietnam

Cronkite Denounces the War

Top left to right: Cronkite interviews a Marine commander during the battle of Hue. ▪ Filming the half-hour news special.

February 27, 1968

Vietnam was the first war fought on television. So it was only fitting that television play an integral role in its resolve.

In 1968 veteran newsman Walter Cronkite, "the most trusted man in America," anchored the *CBS Evening News.* While Cronkite remained neutral on the air, he originally supported the Vietnam War, believing in the domino theory, that if Communists took over Vietnam, all of Asia would fall.

Cronkite visited Saigon early on, attending dinners with high-ranking generals but also visiting the front line. He even went on Air Force bombing raids. In 1964 and 1965, he viewed the American armed forces' effort as impressive. "I was not yet prepared to grasp the fact that Vietnam was no ordinary war as some of us senior correspondents had known it in World War II," he later wrote.

But in 1965 Cronkite started to doubt the military's veracity and the war's likely outcome when he realized the U.S. troop buildup was going to be far larger than the public had originally been told. That year CBS also began airing reports critical of the military's operational conduct. Newsman Morley Safer showed Marines razing a village.

He reported that "this is what the war in Vietnam is all about. The Vietcong were long gone. . . . The action wounded three women, killed one baby, wounded one Marine, and netted four old men as prisoners."

The report angered President Lyndon Johnson, who went so far as to order an investigation of Safer. The coverage showed how television could affect public policy, how the camera could reach people in a way that politicians often couldn't. Soon Cronkite began privately questioning Johnson's handling of the war.

But the veteran news anchor did not see it as his job to guide public opinion, so he did not speak out until 1968 and the Tet offensive, which brought home to television audiences the war and the resilience of the Vietcong.

Cronkite approached Dick Salant, then president of CBS News, and said he wanted to visit Vietnam again, but this time he wanted to take a public stand on the war. It was a risky move but, everyone felt, a necessary one given how divided the nation had become. Cronkite asked to go to Khe Sanh, where the battles were quite intense, but the network couldn't get insurance coverage for such a mission. Instead he went to Hue, where he impressed his younger colleagues with his willingness to wade into the thick of battle for a story.

The news anchor was particularly struck by riding in a helicopter loaded with body bags, especially because this experience was juxtaposed with press briefings in which generals proudly proclaimed that Tet was a definitive victory. He realized that, despite the military's optimism and call for more troops, there was no end in sight. Cronkite returned to New York, and Salant warned him that taking a stand could endanger his reputation and his ratings. But Cronkite was undeterred. On February 27, 1968, he aired a half-hour news special on the Tet offensive but closed the broadcast with an editorial.

While he clearly stated that military victory was an unrealistic goal, Cronkite remained even in tone and relatively balanced, giving him that much more credibility. He started off by reminding viewers that what followed was "speculative, personal, and subjective." Then he commented on the loss of "American lives and dignity" during recent battles as being the "tragedy of our stubbornness there." At one point he clearly yet delicately blamed the government and the military for misleading the public, perhaps his strongest condemnation and a telling blow. "We have been too often disappointed by the optimism of the American leaders both in Vietnam and in Washington and the silver linings they find in the darkest clouds."

He emphasized throughout his commentary that America was neither winning nor losing in Vietnam but was engaged in a grueling, costly standoff. "I'm more certain than ever that the bloody experience of Vietnam is to end in a stalemate." In his strongest language, and with perhaps the only bit of hyperbole, he cautioned that allowing further troop buildups was a recipe for disaster. "With each escalation the world comes closer to the brink of cosmic disaster."

He ended by stating again that negotiations were the only way out of Vietnam, something the government would take another five years to learn. "To say that we are closer to victory today is to believe, in the face of the evidence, the optimists who have been wrong in the past. To suggest we are on the edge of defeat is to yield to unreasonable pessimism. To say that we are mired in stalemate seems the only realistic, yet unsatisfactory, conclusion. . . . It is increasingly clear to this reporter that the only rational way out, then, will be to negotiate, not as victors but as an honorable people who lived up to their pledge to defend democracy, and did the best they could. This is Walter Cronkite. Good night."

The network was surprised that they were not deluged with complaints. But that was either a true indication of public opinion or an endorsement of viewers' trust in their anchorman. President Johnson, who respected Cronkite as

Left to right: Cronkite closed the show with an editorial denouncing the war. ■ On March 31, 1968, Lyndon Johnson announced to a stunned nation that he would not seek reelection to the presidency.

he did no other television news figure, certainly saw it that way, flipping off the set and stating, "If I've lost Cronkite, I've lost middle America."

In fact, losing Cronkite and the support of *Time* magazine nearly simultaneously convinced Johnson to make a startling television delivery of his own just over a month later. On March 31, 1968, the president gave a speech about the nation's involvement in the war, then suddenly—to the surprise of virtually everyone—declared he would not run for reelection. "I shall not seek and I will not accept the nomination of my party as your president."

It is uncertain whether Johnson actually shared Cronkite's assessment of the country's quagmire in Vietnam, or whether

"If I've lost Cronkite, I've lost middle America."

the revered anchor's comments simply became the final straw in Johnson's own appraisal of his chances for reelection. What is certain is that Vietnam showed what an emotionally explosive combination television and war could be. And, as David Halberstam wrote in his book *Powers That Be*, "It was the first time in history that an anchor had declared a war over."

Television in Space

Left to right: Neil Armstrong plants his boot firmly on the lunar surface. ■ Crowds in New York's Grand Central Station watch Glenn's launching in 1962. ■ John Glenn in a training capsule prior to becoming the first American to orbit the earth.

February 20, 1962, July 20, 1969, and January 28, 1986

They had all the elements of an epic miniseries—life-and-death drama, extraordinary heroism, and breathtaking imagery. The larger-than-life qualities of manned flights into space were perfectly suited to the small screen.

Despite the Soviet Union's decisive lead in 1962, President John F. Kennedy understood the military, scientific, and public relations advantages of competing in the space race. He vowed to put a man on the moon by the end of the decade, and television played an unwitting yet invaluable role in making the dream come true.

CBS News producer Don Hewitt intimated that a quid pro quo existed: As long as television coverage helped NASA continue to receive its Congressional appropriations, NASA would continue to provide television with spectacular programs.

On February 20, 1962, astronaut John Glenn, with his all-American leading-man good looks and charm, courageously climbed into his Mercury capsule, dubbed *Friendship 7*, and became the first American astronaut to orbit the earth. In a mission that lasted four hours and 55 minutes, televised from blastoff to splashdown, America had its first space-age superstar.

To make viewers feel as if they were part of the event, Hewitt had a huge television screen hung in Grand Central Station. Periodically through the CBS telecast, he would cut to the crowd gathered in front of the large screen. "The guy at home realized, 'Hey, there are other people as interested in this as I am,'" Hewitt thought.

As *Apollo 11* lifted off on July 16, 1969, "It was as if you could have stood on the dock and waved good-bye to Columbus," said Walter Cronkite, anchorman for the CBS

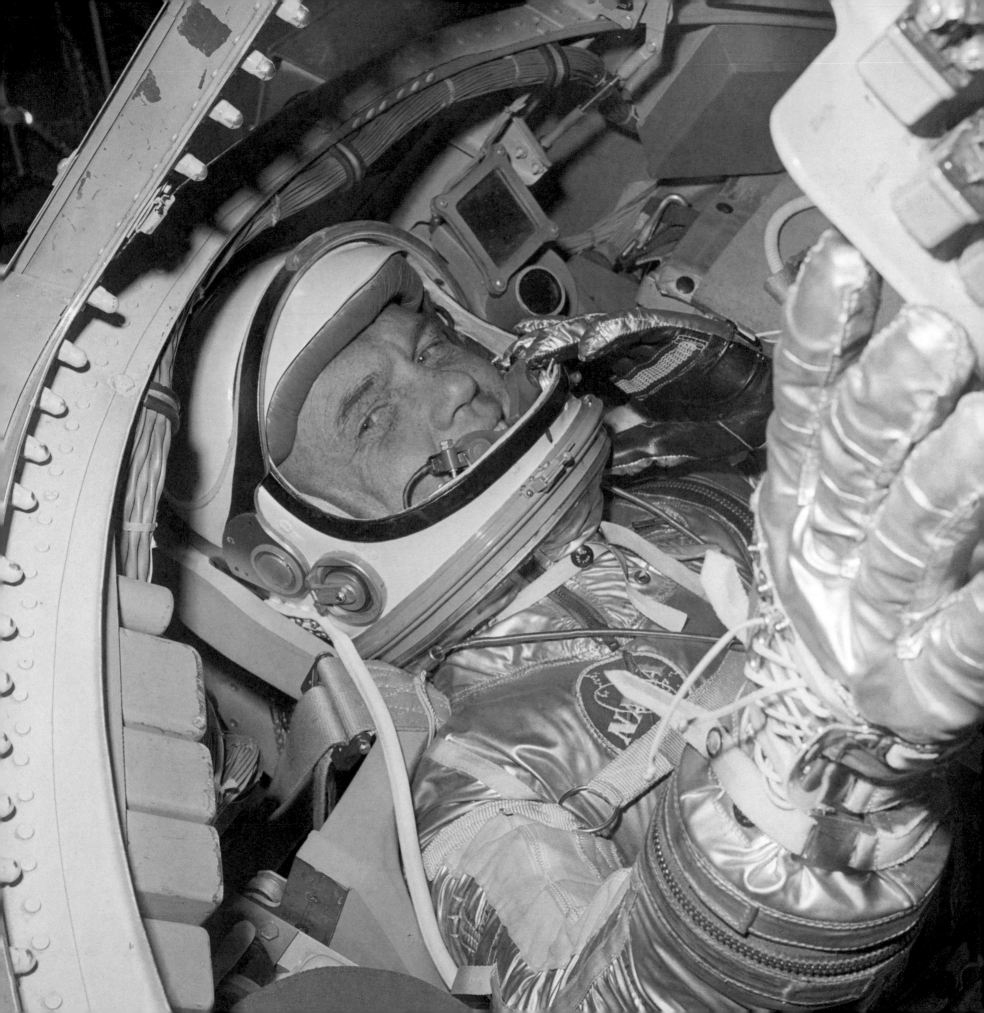

telecast and the man the *New York Times* had dubbed "a one-man phenomenon in space coverage." When Neil Armstrong reported, "The *Eagle* has landed," it marked the culmination of a decade of research, effort, and dreams. The networks had hours to fill—CBS and NBC covered nothing else for 31 straight hours and ABC for 30—and nothing to show, since Armstrong and Edwin "Buzz" Aldrin wouldn't be seen until Armstrong climbed down the ladder and activated the television camera.

Anchoring for ABC were Frank Reynolds and Jules Bergman; NBC had Chet Huntley, David Brinkley, and Frank McGee; and CBS had Walter Cronkite and astronaut Wally Schirra. The networks spent over five million dollars combined coming up with ways to tell the story of the lunar landing.

"I'm just trying to hold on to my breath. This is really something."

Left to right: Apollo 11 *crew members led by Neil Armstrong head for the rocket launch.* ■ Apollo 11 *blastoff to the moon.* ■ *Astronaut Edwin "Buzz" Aldrin prepares to deploy the scientific package.* ■ *Armstrong and Aldrin plant the U.S. flag on the lunar surface.* ■ Apollo 11 *splashdown in the Pacific.*

Each of the three networks had a full-size LM (lunar module) built by Grumman Aircraft Engineering and employed actual astronauts to simulate some of the action, such as Armstrong's descent from the module. ABC and NBC used their own studios, but CBS put theirs in a hangar at Grumman's Long Island plant and built around it a fake moonscape. The networks also had maps of the moon's surface and smaller models of the spaceship and the astronauts' equipment.

When Armstrong climbed down the steps, he activated the seven-pound, $400,000 camera, which beamed its signal through space to Parkes, Australia, from where it was relayed around the world. Suddenly everyone could see a man on the moon. Exhilarated by what he was watching,

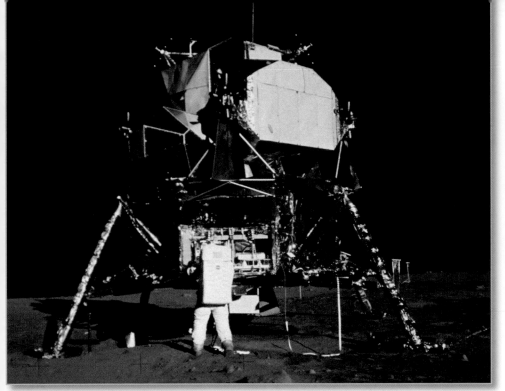

Cronkite desperately tried to maintain his composure. He was seen rubbing his hands nervously and grinning. After 17 straight hours on the air, all he could manage was an "Oh, boy." Then he beckoned his equally awestruck cocommentator, Schirra, to help him out, "Wally, say something, I'm speechless." Schirra responded with "I'm just trying to hold on to my breath. This is really something."

Armstrong made history with his "one small step for man, one giant leap for mankind"; then Aldrin came down and the two men took out an American flag, spoke to President Richard Nixon, posed and bounced around a bit for the television cameras, and got to work exploring the moon.

Television continued to play a central role in the way this experience was shared. While it was a singularly American moment, it captivated the whole world: 600 million people, one-fifth of the earth's population, were watching. In London, people crowded into Trafalgar Square to watch. In Nevada, casinos broke with tradition and set up color TVs in the gambling rooms, asking people to "refrain from their pursuit of jackpots" during the spaceship's approach.

By the time the space shuttle *Challenger* lifted off at 11:38 A.M. EST on January 28, 1986, America felt very different about space exploration. Missions were more frequent and, consequently, the nation and the networks had grown complacent about the space program. Even with the added hoopla NASA had courted by sending the first civilian—New Hampshire schoolteacher Christa McAuliffe—into space, the broadcast networks weren't covering the launch live. Anchors for ABC and NBC were in Washington, D.C., for background briefings on President Ronald Reagan's State of the Union message that evening. While NBC's *Today* show broadcast the liftoff live on the West Coast, it was up to CNN, still a relatively young cable network, to carry the event nationwide.

But 73 seconds into the *Challenger*'s flight, everything changed. Against the deep blue sky, a fiery plume appeared, followed by an explosion and thick white smoke, with tendrils shooting off into the sky. A disembodied official voice announced dryly, "Obviously a major malfunction," followed shortly by, "We have a report from the flight dynamics officer that the vehicle has exploded." It was a catastrophe occurring before a national audience that included students watching to see a teacher enter outer space.

Left to right: The Challenger *lifts off.* ■ *A thick cloud follows the explosion of the space shuttle.* ■ *Spectators at Kennedy Space Center react with horror.* ■ *Students at Marian High School in Framingham, Massachusetts, appear stunned by the shocking telecast.* ■ *Schoolteacher Christa McAuliffe, a Framingham native, died in the disaster with the rest of the crew.* ■ *President Reagan and wife, Nancy, attend a memorial service for the crew of the* Challenger.

The $1.2 billion spacecraft was done in by a $900 synthetic rubber band called an O-ring. Engineers had warned NASA that temperatures below 51 degrees could be dangerous, and it was only 36 degrees that morning. The company that made the O-rings, Morton Thiokol, and NASA ultimately paid multimillion-dollar settlements.

The networks immediately summoned their anchors, knowing that even without much information, they needed them on the air as the nation tried to make sense of what it had just witnessed.

At 11:45 A.M. EST, CBS's Dan Rather was first on the air, rushing without makeup or his contact lenses into the network's "flash studio," where cameras and microphones are immediately available. Rather was ultimately on for five and a half hours. ABC's Peter Jennings and NBC's Tom Brokaw, both in Washington, were on the air shortly after noon.

The networks broadcast commercial-free for hours but, given the limited amount of footage available, they all showed the same horrific images over and over, searing them into our national consciousness. There was, of course, the explosion itself, shown frame by frame. Then there was cheerier footage of McAuliffe and the other astronauts, and the reactions of McAuliffe's parents in Florida and high school students in Concord, New Hampshire, as they watched and realized what had happened.

There were no real answers that day. Rather, who used a two-foot model of the *Challenger* to explain what had happened, pointed out during one replay that there was a tiny explosion on the right rocket booster. CBS also brought on test pilot Leo Krupp to analyze the replays, while ABC had former astronaut Gene Cernan on. Still, Jennings remarked to viewers, "We're in the dark as much as you are."

And so the newscasts were left to do what they could to ease the pain and confusion. NBC had a child psychologist on to give advice to parents on talking with their children about the tragedy. Rather narrated a poem by a former astronaut over footage of the *Challenger* crew getting ready. At another point he quoted an old sailor's expression: "Thy sea is so great, and my boat so small."

President Reagan canceled his State of the Union address, instead choosing to speak to the grief-stricken nation, and specifically the children. "I want to say something to the schoolchildren of America who were watching the live coverage of the shuttle's takeoff. I know it is hard to understand, but sometimes, painful things like this happen. It's all part of the process of exploration and discovery. It's all part of taking a chance and expanding man's horizons. The future doesn't belong to the fainthearted; it belongs to the brave. The *Challenger* crew was pulling us into the future, and we'll continue to follow them."

The nation would never again view manned space flight the same way, having witnessed both its triumph and its tragedy live on television.

Nixon
From Watergate to Resignation

Left top to right: The Watergate Hotel, scene of the burglary of the Democratic National Committee Headquarters. ▪ Nixon addressing the nation about the tapes. ▪ Senate Watergate Committee Chairman Sam Ervin listens to a witness at the nationally televised hearings.

June 17, 1972, to August 8, 1974

It was one of the darkest periods in American political history, and it all played out on television.

It began June 17, 1972, with reports of a break-in at the Democratic National Headquarters in the Watergate Hotel in Washington, D.C. With a large police photo of one of the "burglars," James McCord, appearing on the screen behind him, NBC's Garrick Utley opened his report, "This is James W. McCord, one of five persons surprised and arrested yesterday inside the headquarters of the Democratic National Committee in Washington. McCord is a former CIA employee. Now he runs his own private security service." Then, in an obviously incredulous tone, Utley said, "And guess what else he is—a consultant to President Richard Nixon's reelection campaign committee. Police say McCord and his accomplices brought electronic listening devices with them and had removed two ceiling panels from the office of Democratic National Chairman Lawrence O'Brien." Utley finished with a prophetic aside, "I don't think that's the last we're going to hear of this story."

Ron Ziegler, Nixon's press secretary, immediately began distancing the administration from the episode, saying dis-missively, "I'm not going to comment from the White House on a third-rate burglary incident. We don't condone that kind of second-rate activity." Meanwhile, though, O'Brien continued to push for an investigation, spurred on by reports in the *Washington Post* and then the *New York Times* of an ever-widening web of Watergate-related criminal activity.

On August 30, 1972, Nixon claimed that an investigation into the affair, conducted by White House counsel John Dean, had concluded that there was no link to anyone in the administration. Less than a month later, indictments were handed down against the five Watergate burglars, plus Nixon aides E. Howard Hunt and G. Gordon Liddy, who were accused of masterminding the break-in.

While the Watergate story continued to simmer, the television networks focused on the campaigns, the national party conventions, and the presidential election. In November, Nixon won reelection in a landslide, taking every state except Massachusetts and the District of Columbia, accumulating a total of 520 electoral votes, leaving Senator George McGovern with 17.

Meanwhile, evidence of a conspiracy in the Watergate break-in continued to mount, and the investigation drew

ever closer to the White House. By the following February, the Senate had unanimously voted to impanel the Senate Select Committee on Presidential Campaign Activities, chaired by the Democratic senator from North Carolina, Sam Ervin. On May 18, 1973, Ervin, a self-described "old country lawyer," with a deep southern drawl and expressive bushy eyebrows, began what soon became known as the Watergate hearings.

For the first five days, all three television networks, ABC, CBS, and NBC, covered the hearings gavel to gavel, averaging five hours of airtime per day. Then they agreed on a schedule by which each network would cover the proceedings every third day. But when former White House counsel John Dean appeared before the committee, all three networks elected to broadcast the nearly 30 hours of testimony. In an emotionless monotone, Dean read a carefully written, detailed statement, recalling specific conversations with various members of the administration, including the president, and the nation was riveted. It was reported

versations. In a nationally televised address, he admitted that, taken out of context, some of the material might seem damaging, but considered in its totality it would exonerate him of any wrongdoing. The president had hoped this move would placate his detractors, but ultimately his plan backfired. The television and radio networks dramatized the transcribed conversations, hiring actors or showing photographs of the real people as the excerpts were read on the air. Nixon and his administration were seen as conniving, distrustful, and profane, a veritable snake pit of corruption.

One by one the president's closest advisers were implicated, indicted, and convicted for their parts in the Watergate affair. When the Supreme Court voted unanimously to order the White House to turn over

Left to right: Watergate bugging conspirator James McCord testifies about the bugging device in the phones at the Democratic National Committee Headquarters. ▪ Attorney General John Mitchell absorbs a question posed by members of the Senate committee. ▪ Former presidential aide John Ehrlichman testifies before the committee. ▪ New York customers and employees in a department store television section watch the committee hearings. ▪ H. R. Haldeman takes the oath before testifying. ▪ Senator Ervin confers with colleagues during the hearings.

that 85 percent of U.S. households had tuned in to part or all of the hearings. The daytime Nielsen ratings for the week of July 9 through 13, 1973, placed the Watergate hearings in three of the survey's top 10 slots; NBC was number one for its telecast of the hearings, with a 10.7 rating, barely edging out the circuslike game show *Let's Make a Deal* with its 10.0. The Watergate hearings were number three on ABC with a 9.6 and number eight on CBS with a 9.1, right behind another CBS daytime drama, *As the World Turns*.

When it was revealed during the July testimony of former Nixon aide Alexander Butterfield that a voice-activated taping system had been recording Oval Office conversations dating back to 1971, the hearings took an irreversible turn. As quickly as the committee and the grand jury subpoenaed the tapes, Nixon stonewalled.

After months of battling in the courts, in a preemptive move Nixon said he would make public edited transcripts of the requested con-

sound levels and light placement. A prebroadcast network pool feed recorded the exceedingly uncomfortable scene. In a desperate attempt to lighten the mood, Nixon tried to be funny. To a technician who had just adjusted the microphone, he said, "Hey, you're better lookin' than I am, why don't you stay here, heh?" No one laughed. And, indeed, the president could not break the somber mood. He tried again as the White House photographer snapped shots of him.

Then it came time to adjust the microphone level. Nixon picked up a stack of papers—the resignation speech—looked at it for a long moment, and said, "Guess I can see it." Then he looked up. "Oh, you need to have a level, don't you? Yes, yes," and read the opening to the speech. "Good evening. This is the 37th time I have spoken to you from this office, where so many decisions have been made that shaped the history of our nation." The sound technician told the president, "That's fine," and Nixon stopped reading.

the subpoenaed tapes once and for all, Nixon's presidency permanently unraveled. Among the tapes was a June 23, 1972, conversation in which Nixon and his aide H. R. Haldeman discussed details of Attorney General John Mitchell's involvement and bringing in the CIA for cover. The conversation, which took place six days before Nixon asserted he knew nothing about the break-in, became the "smoking gun."

While the hearings scored high in the ratings, Nixon's approval rating plummeted. Following the January ceasefire in Vietnam, a Gallup poll had placed it at 68 percent. By August, as little doubt remained of the president's involvement in Watergate, his rating had sunk to 30 percent.

With Congress considering an order of impeachment, and a national outcry for his removal from office, Nixon decided that his only choice was resignation. As he prepared for the worldwide radio and television broadcast, the weight of the situation finally got to him. It has been reported that while his TV makeup was being applied, Nixon, who once said, "I never cry, except in public," began openly to weep. When his makeup was finished, he pulled himself together and entered the Oval Office looking reasonably composed. He was still sniffling, but he tried to explain away the congestion as the remnants of a cold.

The Oval Office was crowded with crews from the networks and members of Nixon's staff. The president sat down behind the desk for last-minute adjustments to the

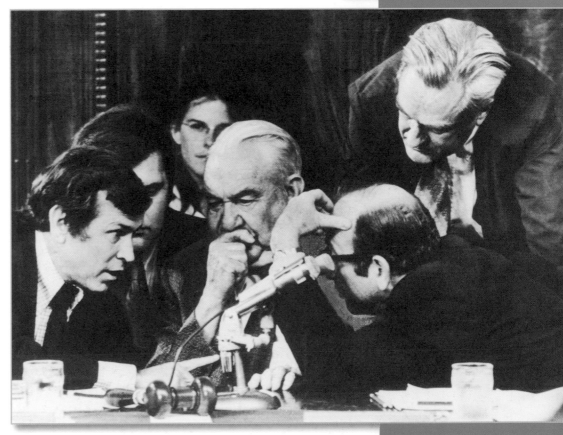

In a desperate attempt to lighten the mood, Nixon tried to be funny.

Left to right: Journalists surround John Ehrlichman as he leaves U. S. District Court after being sentenced. ▪ Nixon and Ford discuss the transfer of the presidency. ▪ Nixon bids farewell to his Cabinet, aides, and staff. ▪ The Nixons say goodbye to the Fords before boarding the helicopter. ▪ Nixon's final salute to the watching viewers.

After a couple more adjustments, and a few more photographs, the president stood up and walked off camera. Two minutes later he was back in the chair, on the air, live, to the nation and the world. The speech lasted approximately 16 minutes, during which Nixon outlined his accomplishments in office, his personal philosophy, and his reasons for resigning. He explained that he wanted to fight the accusations but that doing so would not be in the national interest—it would take up too much of his time and prevent him from governing effectively. Then, with a hint of disbelief in his voice, he read the key sentence in the speech: "Therefore, I shall resign the presidency effective at noon tomorrow."

The next day Nixon delivered a heartfelt speech to his loyal staff and departed the White House grounds via the presidential helicopter. Television cameras were present, in spite of Mrs. Nixon's protest earlier that morning. The president paused in the helicopter's doorway for one of the

most famous photographs ever taken of him—he is smiling, his arms raised, the fingers of each hand extended in a V-formation, looking for all the world like someone who had just won an election, not the first president in U.S. history to resign his office. Shortly before noon on August 9, 1974, Vice President Gerald R. Ford was sworn in as president. A month later, on September 8, 1974, in a surprise move, Ford granted Richard Nixon a "full and absolute" pardon for "all offenses against the United States" committed between January 20, 1969, and August 9, 1974.

In 1952 Richard Nixon had harnessed the power of television to save his career. Twenty-two years later television was there to chronicle his political self-destruction.

Nixon

The TV Princess

Left to right: In 1981 the royal wedding was an international media event. ■ The young royal family with Princes William and Harry.

July 29, 1981, to September 6, 1997

Diana Spencer was born into royalty, and married Britain's future king, but it was television that made her the "People's Princess."

Long before Diana's reign, when monarchies still governed, subjects could live their entire lives without viewing their king or queen. But television changed all that. In England the watershed moment came with the televised coronation of Elizabeth II in 1953. Up until that time the British royal family had believed that appearing on television was undignified and had allowed themselves to be televised only at a distance during official ceremonies. Traditionalists, including Sir Winston Churchill, the Archbishop of Canterbury, and many members of the British government, were aghast at the suggestion that television be allowed to impose on the solemn ceremony.

It was Princess Elizabeth herself who insisted that her ascendancy be televised to Britain. The broadcast was a significant success for the BBC. Five cameras were used in Westminster Abbey, with commentary provided by renowned British broadcaster Richard Dimbleby. The combination of pageantry and the fairy-tale ceremony assured a television triumph.

As time went on, the British royals became more ubiquitous on television. The queen's appearances were mostly official, whereas other members of the royal family inched closer to tabloid fodder. Television did have a humanizing effect on Britain's royals. However, they appeared stiff and sometimes inappropriate, shattering a few myths and recasting themselves as all too fallible.

Until Diana.

Lady Diana Spencer started dating Prince Charles, heir to the British throne, when she was just 17 years old. As the daughter of the Earl of Spencer, she had played with Charles's younger siblings, and Charles had briefly dated her older sister. He was 12 years her senior, but the differences between the two were more than mere years. Diana was perceived as everything Charles and his family were not; whereas they were stuffy traditionalists, she was warm, open, and charismatic. Diana was also beautiful, and the camera loved her.

Charles and Diana were married on July 29, 1981, in St. Paul's Cathedral in a televised spectacle that included all

the opulence and pageantry befitting such an occasion, and nearly three quarters of a billion people tuned in. Just a year earlier she had been working at a kindergarten in London. Now Diana was the Princess of Wales.

Their life together was a public one, a blade with two edges. On the one hand, Diana was a natural, displaying grace whether she was at a ribbon-cutting ceremony or appearing with her children. (Prince William was born a year after the wedding and his brother, Prince Harry, two years later.) But she was pursued, even stalked, by the press. And though she asked to be left alone—particularly when she was with her children—the request was ignored. The attention took its toll on her marriage.

Left to right: Diana was a devoted mother to her two sons. ▪ After her divorce, Diana began a relationship with wealthy Egyptian businessmanDodi Al Fayed. ▪ The scene of the horrific high-speed collision in the tunnel. ▪ Ambulances on the scene were unable to save the princess, and only the bodyguard survived the crash.

After seemingly endless revelations of adultery, in 1992 Prime Minister John Major announced that Charles and Diana were separating, and the two became a daily topic for the media. Ultimately, Charles would admit to his marital transgressions in a televised documentary. Diana, who knew the value of television whether she was getting attention for her many causes or lashing out at her in-laws, responded in a 1995 TV interview detailing her own affairs and bouts with depression and bulimia, and accused the royal family of being uncaring. The interview infuriated the queen, who then urged her son to get a divorce. The storybook snapped shut in 1996.

After her divorce Diana worked at being a mother and became a high-profile spokesperson in the fight to rid the world of land mines. Though she might have enjoyed more privacy elsewhere, she remained in Britain as the hands-on mother to her two princes. She was determined that they have as much normalcy as possible within the invisible bars of British royal life.

Diana began a relationship with a jet-setting Egyptian businessman named Dodi Al Fayed. On the night of August 30, 1997, the pair

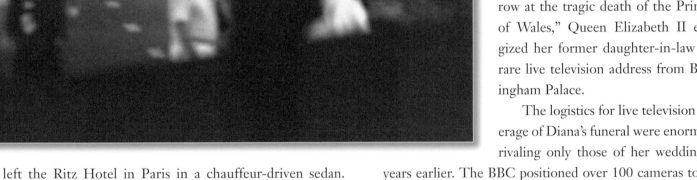

left the Ritz Hotel in Paris in a chauffeur-driven sedan. The car was pursued by paparazzi on motorcycles, desperate to get a picture of the two. Fayed's driver lost control, and the sedan careened into a pillar, killing the driver and Fayed instantly. Diana died a few hours later in a French hospital. In an oft reported quote, her brother said, "This is not a time for recriminations but for sadness. However, I would say that I always believed the press would kill her in the end. But not even I could imagine that they would take such a direct hand in her death, as seems to be the case."

Diana's death sent a shock wave around the world. CNN, the worldwide television news channel, reported that more viewers tuned in for their coverage of the death of Diana than had watched coverage of China's Tiananmen Square uprising, the fall of the Berlin Wall, or the 1996 Atlanta Olympic Park bombing.

In an effort to stave off the criticism that the royal fam-

ily was "indifferent to the country's sorrow at the tragic death of the Princess of Wales," Queen Elizabeth II eulogized her former daughter-in-law in a rare live television address from Buckingham Palace.

The logistics for live television coverage of Diana's funeral were enormous, rivaling only those of her wedding 16 years earlier. The BBC positioned over 100 cameras to follow the procession through the streets of London to Westminster Abbey, then to her private burial site at the Spencer family home in Althorp. David Dimbleby, whose father had narrated Elizabeth II's first royal telecast, provided the commentary for Diana's funeral.

Like her wedding, Diana's funeral drew an international audience, though this time the tears were sad, not joyful. On September 6, 1997, the whole world watched as her casket was driven on a carriage through London. They watched as the procession stopped in front of Buckingham Palace, saw the queen and her family standing solemnly at the gate. Diana's sons, Prince Charles, the Duke of Edinburgh, and Diana's brother walked behind the carriage to the abbey. The world cried along with her family as Elton John sang a reworked version of "Candle in the Wind," in tribute to his friend Diana.

Like her wedding, Diana's funeral drew an international audience.

As the hearse headed for Diana's family home, Dimbleby offered a poignant farewell: "Diana memorably said that she wanted to be a queen in people's hearts, and what we are witnessing is the coronation of that queen."

Diana lived and died a public life. Her legacy is in many ways a product of television. As modern media helped create the spectacle that was her life, they also perhaps contributed to the tragedy that was her death.

Left to right: The Duke of Edinburgh, Prince William, the Ninth Earl of Spencer, Prince Harry and the Prince of Wales at Diana's funeral. ▪ Queen Elizabeth pays tribute to Diana, speaking on television from Buckingham Palace. ▪ Diana's coffin is carried out of Westminster following the funeral service. ▪ Elton John performs "Candle in the Wind" at the funeral. ▪ Mourners watched on a giant video screen in Hyde Park as the casket is carried into the abbey. ▪ Diana's brother Earl Charles Spencer addresses the congregation during his sister's funeral service.

The Rescue of Baby Jessica

October 14–16, 1987

One minute, 18-month-old Jessica McClure was an anonymous little girl. The next, she was everybody's baby—trapped 22 feet down an abandoned well, cold and dark, save for the hot spotlight of local rescuers, and worldwide television.

Jessica McClure fell into the well while playing in the backyard of her aunt's home in Midland, Texas, on October 14, 1987. The hole was eight inches in diameter near the top, narrowing to just six inches, far too small for any rescue worker to enter. Crews arrived soon after she fell—first emergency, then television.

Rescue workers quickly assessed the situation. The only hope of saving little Jessica would be to drill a parallel shaft next to the one she was in, then tunnel across and pull her through. In a matter of hours the plight of "baby Jessica" was being broadcast around the globe via CNN, at that time the nation's only 24-hour cable news network.

Left to right: Jessica's mother waits anxiously, holding the baby's teddy bear. ▪ As the only 24-hour news network, CNN took the lead in round-the-clock coverage of the rescue. ▪ The rescue team at work.

CNN's Tony Clark said their first challenge was to fight through the large group of onlookers that had gathered at the fence surrounding the yard. "As soon as the crew and I got there, we went knocking on doors to get a ladder just to be able to see over the fence to shoot video of the rescue effort." As other members of the media arrived,

Voice of
Tony Clark
Midland, Texas

CNN LIVE

each with a ladder taller than the one in front, the area began to resemble a grandstand full of lights, news cameras, and still photographers.

Viewers quickly learned that Jessica's mother was visiting her sister when she stepped away from her daughter to answer the phone. It was at that exact moment that Jessica fell into the well.

As the drama unfolded, the cast of characters became household figures. There were Jessica's terrified teenage parents, Chip and Cissy, and the official spokesman for the operation, Midland Police Chief Richard Czech. There were the paramedics Steve Forbes and Robert O'Donnell, the pair who would eventually pull Jessica to safety. There was the town of Midland itself, an oil town suffering through an economic slump, a Texas community brought together as volunteers and local construction workers descended on the rescue scene. Midland's unified effort to save Jessica became as much a part of the story as the rescue itself.

As the hours mounted and progress was measured only in inches, CNN's Greg LaMotte began to grow skeptical of Jessica's chances for survival. "When I first heard about it, I thought, 'I'm sure they'll have her out in a few hours, no problem.' Then, as a few hours turned into 10 hours, and 11 hours, and 12 hours, . . . I began to think, 'She isn't going to make it.'"

But for the time being, Jessica was alive. Sometimes she was heard singing, humming, and occasionally crying. She was comforted by the sounds of Winnie-the-Pooh and Humpty Dumpty songs piped down to her, along with oxygen that was warmed at night as temperatures fell into the 50s.

During the first day, viewers felt the frustration of the construction workers, whose drilling was going at an agonizingly slow pace. Then Chief Czech told reporters, "It seems like we might be on the right course to the girl, but it will be several more hours."

The story of the helpless child gripped the nation, and offers of assistance poured in from every corner. The turning point in the rescue effort came when a company in Tennessee offered the use of their specialized high-pressure water drill, capable of drilling through the nearly impenetrable rock that had become Jessica's prison. The drill was flown to Midland and immediately put to use.

As night fell on a second day of nonstop drilling, hope began to rise. "We're told that two paramedics are now down in the shaft," LaMotte reported to a world on the edge of its seat. "It may be just a matter of time now before they're able to pull young Jessica out."

Earl Maple was directing the network's coverage from the CNN Center in Atlanta. As the rescue cables began to rise out of the parallel shaft, Maple instructed Clark to "let the pictures tell the story."

When cameras caught Jessica emerging from the well,

"Clearly this was one of those stories that you rarely get a chance to cover in your life— of something extraordinarily positive happening."

Taking advantage of the TV cameras still trained on the celebration, grateful rescue workers decided to express their gratitude to the viewing audience. They held up a homemade cardboard sign that read simply THANK YOU, AMERICA.

"Clearly this was one of those stories that you rarely get a chance to cover in your life—of something extraordinarily positive happening," recalls LaMotte, "watching mankind help itself."

But the television story didn't end there. In 1989 Jessica's ordeal became the subject of a made-for-TV movie titled *Everybody's Baby: The Rescue of Jessica McClure.*

As in times of great tragedy and triumph throughout TV's history, television became the hearth for a worldwide audience to gather in common concern and hope for a helpless child, bearing witness to what television does best.

viewers heard the eruption of cheers from the rescue workers and volunteers. Then they got their first glimpse of baby Jessica. "When she came out," Maple recalls, "everybody in the control room let out a sigh of relief. It was very emotional."

Jessica emerged from the well drowsy and three pounds lighter. Despite a badly damaged foot, she was alive, the answered prayer of her anxious parents, exhausted volunteers, the town of Midland, and the worldwide audience. She was immediately taken to an awaiting ambulance, and reports said she began feeling better soon after eating an orange Popsicle in the hospital. Jessica eventually lost three toes.

Left to right: Scores of rescuers worked to dig a shaft adjacent to the well, while millions of Americans watched the drama on television. ∎ *The ordeal was terrifying for Jessica's parents.* ∎ *Robert O'Donnell emerges from the well with Jessica safely in his arms.* ∎ *A rescue worker holds up a new homemade cover for the water pipe Jessica fell into.*

The Fall of the Berlin Wall

November 9, 1989

I n an article for *TV Guide*, Walter Cronkite said that as a television reporter, his most vivid memories are of covering the Kennedy assassination and the *Apollo 11* moon landing. But as a viewer, the most dramatic scenes he ever witnessed were of the fall of the Berlin Wall. "The heroism of those people taking the wall down . . . was truly something to behold."

On November 9, 1989, that joyous celebration was televised around the glove. The 96-mile-long, 12-foot-high concrete wall that had divided a city and a people, both physically and ideologically, for 28 years, began to tumble down. Unlike the walls of Jericho, the Berlin Wall wasn't brought down by trumpets; the instruments were wrecking balls, bulldozers, pickaxes, shovels, hammers, chisels, and fingernails—and the will of a people forced to endure over four decades of Soviet oppression.

Though the Berlin Wall was erected in 1961, its foundations go back to World War II. After the fall of the Nazi regime in 1945, the Allies divided Germany into four parts. In the summer of 1945, the Allied powers, represented by Harry Truman of the United States, Winston Churchill of

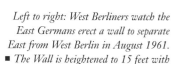

Left to right: West Berliners watch the East Germans erect a wall to separate East from West Berlin in August 1961. ▪ The Wall is heightened to 15 feet with bricks, as a policeman stands guard. ▪ At the Brandenburg Gate, celebrating the new unity.

Great Britain, Charles de Gaulle of France, and Joseph Stalin of the Soviet Union, met for two weeks in Potsdam, Germany, and split up the country. Great Britain, France, and the United States occupied the western half of Germany and the U.S.S.R. the eastern part—which they renamed the German Democratic Republic or G.D.R. Berlin was a special case; even though it lies entirely in East Germany, it too was split in half. In 1949 the western half of the city became known as West Berlin, and the eastern half became the Soviet Sector.

In the 1950s West Germany and West Berlin quickly expanded and modernized. At the same time, East Germans remained trapped in the first half of the century, straitjacketed by their Soviet overlords. The Communist concepts put into place included collective agriculture and repression of private trade, resulting in a lack of basic goods. East

Berlin was sometimes referred to as Mini-Moscow. By comparison, the East Germans' counterparts just across the line were enjoying the fruits of a postwar boom. On June 17, 1953, there was rioting in the streets of East Berlin. But the uprising was short-lived—as the workers gathered at the Brandenburg Gate, Russian tanks rolled up and began firing into the unarmed crowd, which quickly dispersed.

By the time the 1960s rolled around, there was massive dissatisfaction among East German citizens. The political atmosphere was tense as well. In November 1958, Soviet Premier Nikita Khrushchev had delivered an ultimatum—he demanded that the Western Allies withdraw their troops from West Berlin and that it become a "Free City" within six months. All this was designed to stem the flow of people from East to West. In the first eight months of 1961, an estimated 160,000 refugees had left the G.D.R. On Saturday,

August 12, 1961, over 2,000 East German refugees crossed over to the West and applied for asylum. On Sunday, August 13, 1961, that all stopped.

Early that morning the G.D.R. took drastic measures to stem the flow of refugees. As people slept, bulldozers and tanks began a massive task—to construct a wall between East and West Berlin. First came barbed wire and antitank

Over the decades almost a hundred people died attempting to escape to the West to live in freedom.

obstacles. Then streets were torn up and stone barricades erected. Platoons of Russian soldiers stood guard as tanks patrolled crucial intersections. Rail and subway lines were interrupted. Beginning that day the citizens of East and West Berlin were no longer permitted free access to one another. In one day the 80 crossing points in the city had been reduced to a mere 13. In the following days battalions of construction workers began replacing the temporary blockades with a concrete wall. Before August 13, 60,000 commuters had crossed the border to work in West Berlin each weekday. Only a handful of refugees got across the border that day—most by stealing through the basements of houses that lay on the line. And a number of East Berliners who worked the night shift in West Berlin were stranded.

In June 1963 American President John F. Kennedy, speaking at the Berlin Wall, expressed solidarity with the

Left: President John Kennedy looks at the Berlin Wall just before his famous "Ich bin ein Berliner" speech on June 26, 1963. Right: President Reagan used the setting of the Brandenburg Gate to demand that Russian leader Gorbachev "tear down this wall" on June 12, 1987. ■ On November 10, 1989, the world watched as Berliners chipped and hammered and gouged at the hated symbol.

GENERAL SECRETARY GORBACHEV, IF YOU
SEEK PEACE /- IF YOU SEEK PROSPERITY FOR
THE SOVIET UNION AND EASTERN EUROPE /-
IF YOU SEEK LIBERALIZATION! COME HERE,
TO THIS GATE.

MR. GORBACHEV, OPEN THIS GATE.
MR. GORBACHEV, TEAR DOWN THIS WALL.

freedom seekers in his famous "Ich bin ein Berliner" speech. But through the 1970s and into the early 1980s, not much changed. Over the decades almost a hundred people died attempting to escape to the West to live in freedom.

Finally, in the mid-1980s, there appeared a crack in the wall, a crack opened up by new Soviet leader Mikhail Gorbachev and his twin concepts of *perestroika* and *glasnost*. Gorbachev recognized the need for reconstruction in the U.S.S.R.—to bring his crumbling country into the modern age. The cold war had begun to thaw. Little did Gorbachev know that he was presiding over the beginning of the end for the Soviet Union and the Eastern Bloc.

In 1989 emigration laws in Europe began to ease. Hungary opened its borders, and a mass departure from the G.D.R. began. By October thousands of East German

citizens—a large percentage of them young people—had abandoned their country. On October 9, two days after the 40th anniversary of the G.D.R., thousands of protesters massed in the streets of East Berlin, chanting slogans of peace and German reunifica-
tion. By October 16 they num-
bered in the millions and issued
a statement: "We have worked
our fingers to the bone for this
country, and we are not standing by to see it all fall into ruins.
The truth has come to light—a
nation that cannot keep their
young at home has no future."

On November 9, the East
German government simply
gave in. In a television broadcast
they took the world by surprise
by announcing new regulations:
East German citizens could now travel to the West without restriction. The wall was open, and an exodus of biblical proportions began. Berlin's main artery, the Kurfürstendamm, was so packed with foot traffic it had to be closed to vehicles.

The BBC Television's Graham Leach, reporting live at the scene breathlessly tried to take it all in: "These are truly remarkable scenes taking place here tonight on the eastern side of the Berlin Wall at Checkpoint Charlie. Hundreds of people have gathered here in the hope of getting across . . . through the Berlin Wall and across the frontier between the two Germanys. In the distance . . . I can see numerous flashlights . . . ordinary people who have turned out in the hundreds just to be here on this historic evening. People on the [western] side are chanting, urging people on this side to come across."

Police at Checkpoint Charlie finally gave up trying to check documents, letting the people flood through the gate— and there were a huge number of West Berliners waiting to greet the East German arrivals. Champagne bottles were uncorked—the first East German to make it across was raised aloft by the crowd and showered with champagne.

Then, on the evening of November 10, as the world watched, the first concrete slab was removed from the wall to the cheering of thousands of East and West Berliners. But

As the photos on these pages record, East and West Berliners shouted and sang with joy as they crossed over the newly opened border. Far right top: Three original slabs of the Berlin Wall are being used in a monument at Fort Leavenworth, Kansas, in recognition of the historic destruction of the infamous structure.

it wasn't just heavy machinery taking down the wall. People all along the graffitied wall, dubbed "wall woodpeckers," were chipping away at it with whatever tools they could find. Pieces of the wall were highly prized—and tons of that concrete, in the form of tiny chunks packaged in plastic, would make its way into souvenir shops around the world.

The only American news anchor live on the scene was NBC's Tom Brokaw. Asked about his feelings that night, he

replied, "It was an amazing moment . . . and I felt very privileged to be there. I do remember thinking that night as we were live on the air with *Nightly News* . . . you know, you get very few chances like this in a journalistic career to be at one of the really watershed moments in the changing political dynamic of the world."

Seven months after the wall fell, the East German government toppled, as would the Communist government of Russia. On July 1, 1990, the two Germanys reunited, and few remnants remained of the concrete barrier that had divided the city of Berlin and its people for nearly three decades. In 1998 a 210-foot-long section of the wall was designated a national monument so that the city and the world might never forget, and never repeat this painful history.

Chasing O.J.

June 17, 1994

Left to right: O. J. Simpson's white Ford Bronco slowly makes its way down Interstate 5 with police cars in pursuit.
■ *KCBS in L.A. had exclusive coverage of the chase initially, but soon seven news choppers were tracking the Bronco.*
■ *Alerted by the TV coverage, crowds lined the freeway to catch a glimpse of the celebrity fugitive.*

It wasn't really a chase. It was more like a procession. But America's obsession with celebrity, and the real possibility of a live shoot-out or suicide, made O. J. Simpson's 1994 freeway run perversely riveting. A television spectacle like no other, it completely transformed network programming and drew close to 95 million viewers over the course of the night.

The backdrop is only too well known. After retiring from the NFL in 1979, the former football star parlayed his fame, likable personality, and good looks into a successful career in commercials, movies, and broadcasting. In his free time, O.J. could be found playing on one of Los Angeles's more exclusive golf courses.

But a dark side was revealed. After the murder of Simpson's ex-wife, Nicole, and her friend Ronald Goldman, the media reported rumors of Simpson's penchant for drug use, partying, and womanizing, and the hard, cold facts of his domestic violence record. Nicole Simpson had ended her abusive marriage in 1992. On June 12, 1994, Nicole and Goldman were found brutally murdered outside her Brentwood, California, condominium while the Simpson children were sleeping upstairs.

Evidence gleamed from the murder site suggested O.J. might be the killer. On Friday, June 17, he was to surrender, charged with "willfully, unlawfully, and with malice aforethought murdering Nicole Brown Simpson and Ronald Lyle Goldman." The double murder charge meant no bail and a possible death penalty.

In an unusual move, Simpson's attorneys negotiated for him to turn himself in. The surrender was planned as a care-

fully staged TV event. Simpson was to arrive at 11 A.M., then hold an 11:45 A.M. press conference with prosecutors and, after that, one with police officials. When he didn't show, confusion took hold and the scene was set.

Among the throng of reporters waiting for Simpson at Parker Center were independent journalists Robert and Marika Tur. "We decided we weren't going to stand with the other 1,000 reporters and camera crews and wait for O.J. to give himself up, or wait for the next word from the police department," recalls Robert Tur. "We were going to find him." So the Turs boarded their helicopter and took to the air. "We kind of scoped out the west Los Angeles area really quickly, then went back to Santa Monica Airport," he says.

In the effort to "spin" the bizarre turn of events, the district attorney held an afternoon press conference, as did Simpson's attorney Robert Shapiro, who proclaimed himself shocked and disappointed. Then a friend, Robert

Kardashian, read a rambling letter from Simpson, which said in part, "First everyone understand I had nothing to do with Nicole's murder. . . . If we had a problem it's because I loved her so much. . . . God brought you to me I now see. As I leave, you'll be in my thoughts. . . . Don't feel sorry for me. I've had a great life."

After watching Kardashian read Simpson's note, Marika Tur recalls, "I'm thinking, 'He's committing suicide.' And I'm thinking, 'Where would he go to do it?' West side,

maybe he'd be up in the mountains, overlooking the city, overlooking the ocean. Someplace very beautiful and serene." Robert Tur had another idea. "I thought he'd go down to the grave site of his ex-wife, down in Orange County." Marika concurred. So the Turs headed toward Orange County.

Although police had put out an all points bulletin for Simpson and his companion Al Cowlings at 2 P.M., it wasn't until 6:45 P.M. that Simpson was finally located.

A sheriff's car spotted Simpson's 1993 white Ford Bronco traveling north on Interstate 5, not far from his ex-wife's grave. But when they approached the vehicle, which was caught in a traffic jam, Cowlings yelled that Simpson

siderably north and west of their actual location. Then, with Simpson in their sights, they turned on the cameras, and KCBS had their exclusive. But soon seven news choppers were tracking the Bronco and the numerous police cars.

CBS, ABC, CNN, and even ESPN quickly signed on, bringing out top anchors like Dan Rather and Peter Jennings. NBC—where Simpson worked as an analyst on the NFL telecasts—initially only provided updates during its broadcast of the NBA finals between the New York Knicks and Houston

"This has been the most incredible series of events that we have ever witnessed on a single news story."

Rockets. But at the start of the second half, network president Andrew Lack reportedly called Dick Ebersol, president of NBC Sports, and told him the network was jumping on the caravan. NBC came back to the game for the last few minutes.

Everyone was showing the same image. Anchors were often hard-pressed to add anything of note, resorting to comments like "We can hardly believe what we're seeing" and "This has been the most incredible series of events that we have ever witnessed on a single news story."

Stations rounded up Simpson's friends, hoping he was listening to their radio simulcasts. Jim Hill, a former football player turned KCBS sportscaster, told him to "stand

Left to right: Simpson with his two children and wife Nicole in happier times. ▪ An entourage of police cars trails the Bronco. ▪ Members of the news media watch the live television coverage of the chase during the NBA finals at New York's Madison Square Garden. ▪ Simpson arrived back at his Brentwood home, and filming continued by hovering news choppers.

had a gun to his head, prompting the decision simply to follow the Bronco. So the "chase" was on.

While flying in the direction of the cemetery, the Turs monitored Orange County police radio and learned of the slow-speed pursuit. To throw off the competition, the Turs, working for the local CBS affiliate that day, radioed to the assignment desk that they were headed out to Malibu, con-

up. Be a man. Face the situation." Simpson's college coach John McKay asked him to surrender, adding, "I'll stand by you the rest of my life."

The Bronco arrived back at 360 North Rockingham Avenue, Simpson's Brentwood home, just before 8 P.M. after having inched past television satellite trucks. But Simpson stayed inside for nearly an hour as the sun went down. During the wait, local stations shared broadcast pictures while each chopper refueled. Simpson finally stepped out at around 8:45 P.M. It was discovered that he was carrying family pictures, a passport, a fake goatee and mustache, $8,000 in cash, and a loaded Smith & Wesson .357 Magnum. His

arrest and departure for processing at Park Center happened off-screen.

Of course, the saga of O. J. Simpson didn't end with his surrender. That was just the beginning, a watershed moment in the "tabloidization" of television news. Next came the racially divisive criminal trial. The 133 days of televised testimony bestowed Andy Warhol's prescribed 15 minutes of fame on the witnesses, the prosecution team, the high-priced battery of defense attorneys the press dubbed the Dream Team, and the police detectives. Even the trial judge, Lance Ito, became a much parodied personality. *The Tonight Show* host Jay Leno frequently featured a

chorus line of black-robed Asian men, calling them the Dancing Itos.

After listening to 150 witnesses during eight months of testimony, the jury took just three hours to arrive at a verdict. As America watched, at 10 A.M. PST on October 3, 1995, Ito's court clerk, Deidre Robertson, announced the decision: "We the jury in the above entitled action find the defendant, Orenthal James Simpson, not guilty of the crime of murder."

Simpson was acquitted before an estimated 100 million viewers. The trial that writer Dominick Dunne called "the Super Bowl of murder trials" was over.

Presidential Election Night Coverage 2000

November 7, 2000

E lection day 2000 signaled the beginning of the end of what had been a contentious campaign season between Democrat Vice President Albert Gore and his Republican opponent, Governor George W. Bush of Texas.

On election-day eve, NBC's Tim Russert, who would coanchor the network's election-night coverage with Tom Brokaw, appeared on the *Today* show to give viewers a preview of possible election-day voter scenarios. As the interview drew to a close, *Today* cohost Matt Lauer asked Russert, "What's the key element we should be watching for throughout the day tomorrow?" Russert's prophetic answer: "Florida. Florida. Florida. I honestly believe, Matt, as goes Florida so goes the nation."

"I said that," Russert later asserted,

Left to right: In Kosovo, a U.S. soldier watches results for the still undecided election on November 8. ■ *Five days later, television satellite trucks block the streets in Tallahassee, Florida, where a final tally of votes has yet to be completed.* ■ *Candidate George W. Bush with his father on election night in Austin.*

Woodruff. "CNN announces that we call Florida in the Al Gore column. This is a state both candidates desperately wanted to win." Winning the state of Florida and its 25 electoral votes gave the Gore camp the first big-state momentum of the evening, but it was short-lived.

> "We don't just have egg on our face. . . . We have an entire omelet."

As polls closed across the country, the networks turned their attention away from Florida and continued their conjecture about results in other states. Bush was sweeping the South, while Gore looked to be the winner in Michigan and Pennsylvania. On CBS, Rather asserted that Bush's chance

"because I thought the state of Florida had changed significantly over the last several presidential election cycles. It had voted Democratic, then it switched to Republican. And now I thought the changing demographics in the state were almost a microcosm of the rest of the country." Little did Russert know that his prediction would be the only one to hold up during the long and frustrating television coverage of presidential election 2000.

On Tuesday, November 7, 2000, at 7 P.M. EST, polls closed in 11 states. The Associated Press and the major networks almost immediately predicted Bush the winner in Indiana and Kentucky. Said CBS's Dan Rather, "We would rather be last than be wrong. If we say somebody's carried a state, you can pretty much take it to the bank."

One hour later Voter News Service (VNS), an exit polling service owned by a consortium of the network news departments and the Associated Press, asserted that Gore had won in Florida. Florida, where candidate Bush's brother Jeb was governor, was considered a pivotal state, and its winner would likely become the next president. "A big call to make," declared CNN's Judy

Left to right: TV cameras film observers and volunteer ballot counters in Broward County, Florida, where a manual recount of votes was approved by the state supreme court. ■ *On December 11, supporters of Gore and Bush face off in front of the Supreme Court, where the landmark legal battle was taking place.*

to win the election was now "shakier than cafeteria Jell-O." In fact, what was becoming shaky was the network's prediction of Gore's Florida win.

Tim Russert, who coanchored NBC's election night coverage with Tom Brokaw, recalls, "We began to receive phone calls from the Bush campaign, from the Gore campaign, from people on the ground in Florida, all suggesting this thing is getting tighter and tighter. So, then the pro-

jection for Gore was pulled back." The first real indication that Florida was still in play came from one of the candidates. Addressing the media from his campaign headquarters, Bush said, "The networks called this thing awfully early, but the people actually counting the votes are coming up with a different perspective. So we're pretty darn upbeat about things."

At approximately 10 P.M. EST the VNS recanted—and

Florida was back in play. Brokaw reported that Florida was undecided. "We don't just have egg on our face," he announced. "We have an entire omelet." Around 11 P.M., the phrase "too close to call" had become a permanent part of the political lexicon for the 2000 presidential election coverage.

As Tuesday night became Wednesday morning, the network anchors, particularly Tim Russert with the help of his grease board, were busy giving those still awake a lesson in electoral math. Experts on every channel tried to figure out if the election could be won with Florida undecided.

By about 2:15 A.M. EST on November 8, the VNS advised the networks they were ready to call Florida and the election for Bush. "It was in the wee hours of the morning that we were told in our earpieces again that a projection was imminent, and this time it was going to be for George W. Bush," recalls Russert. "And I remember turning to Tom [Brokaw], and I said, 'I hope they got it right this time.'" "Florida for Bush," Brokaw warily announced. "That would be something if the networks managed to blow it twice in one night."

Resigned to the apparent outcome, Gore called his opponent and wished him well. He then left his Nashville hotel room and headed to a rally to make his public concession speech. The pundits ceased talking about the election and began to discuss the new Bush administration. But before Gore reached the stage, the vote tally in Florida had drawn extremely close. "We got more phone calls saying, 'It's getting tighter and tighter,'" Russert remembers, "and Brokaw said, 'Oh, my God, it's down to 251 votes.'"

Florida, which eight hours earlier had belonged to Gore and only moments before been captured by Bush, was again in play. According to *Time* magazine, Gore called Bush to tell him he had changed his mind about conceding.

Just before daybreak, with only a few hundred votes separating the candidates, Judy Woodruff on CNN admitted that she was at a loss for words. "Florida has gone from too close to call—to Gore—to too close to call—to Bush—back to too close to call. . . . This is truly amazing," she said. At about 4 A.M. the networks began to back off their prediction that Bush had won. "We're not absolutely sure what to do next," said Peter Jennings.

The allocation of electoral votes from the other 49 states meant that the election would be decided by the result in the Sunshine State. The closeness of the vote triggered a Florida statute mandating a recount. On November 9, Gore and his representatives requested a hand count in four Florida counties: Palm Beach, Broward, Volusia, and Dade.

The next day the machine recount was complete, and the Associated Press reported that Bush was ahead by a few hundred votes out of nearly six million cast.

The Florida situation dominated the media. Television gave the country an education in ballot construction, and how chads—"hanging," "dimpled," or "pregnant"—determine the validity of ballots. Much of the controversy was centered in Palm Beach, a traditionally Democratic region where an inordinate amount of votes were cast for Pat Buchanan. It seemed that some voters who intended to vote for Gore were confused by the ballot and were alleging that they had mistakenly voted for the conservative Reform Party candidate.

The election ended up in the courts, seesawing between the state and the federal level, with both the Gore and the Bush camps claiming victory at one time or another. Votes were counted and recounted, recounts were started, then halted. Ultimately, the decision came from the U.S. Supreme Court.

On December 12, 2000, by a vote of 5–4, the Supreme Court, citing Florida's own statute mandating that any election controversy must be decided by December 12, ruled any further recount was unconstitutional. Bush had won Florida and the presidency.

Months after the election, an independent report commissioned by CNN ripped the networks, including CNN,

Left to right: CNN *announces the Supreme Court decision.* ■ *On December 13, Vice President Gore concedes the election and vows to work with his opponent to heal the divisions.* ■ *Outgoing President Clinton departs the White House for the final time with Bush on the way to the inauguration.* ■ *George W. Bush takes the oath of office.* ■ *The new president addresses the crowd.*

and the Voter News Service for their reckless performance during the election night broadcasts. The report asserted that the networks had engaged in a "collective drag race on the crowded highway of democracy." In short, their haste to "be first" had led them to faulty reporting.

And so ended television's longest, and most unpredictable, coverage of an election in modern history.

September 11th

September 11, 2001

Top: A second hijacked plane crashes into the South Tower of the World Trade Center minutes after American Airlines Flight 11 hit the North Tower. ▪ Aaron Brown reports the attack on CNN. ▪ The towers billowed flames, smoke, and debris, and then both succumbed to the intense heat and stress, collapsing completely.

Not since the assassination of President John F. Kennedy in 1963 had television so strongly displayed its awesome ability to join millions of Americans in a common crucible of hope and humanity.

At 8:46 A.M. EST, on September 11, 2001, the network morning news shows broke from their regular programming to report that a plane had crashed into the North Tower of the World Trade Center in Lower Manhattan. Viewers were shown a live picture of the North Tower on fire, a huge hole billowing smoke near the top.

Preliminary speculation suggested that it was a private plane flying too low and off course. Conjecture led information by a wide margin. No one anticipated the horrifying reality that it was American Airlines Flight 11, en route from Boston to Los Angeles, carrying 92 passengers and crew, and 16,000 gallons of explosive jet fuel, deliberately flown into the building.

Then, at 9:06 A.M. EST, with network cameras trained on the burning North Tower, the nation witnessed perhaps the most incredible sight ever broadcast on live television. While everyone was gazing in bewilderment at the burning

North Tower, United Flight 175 came into view and slammed into the South Tower, causing a huge fireball. It was becoming clear that this was no accident. The network anchors—Tom Brokaw of NBC, Dan Rather of CBS, Peter Jennings at ABC, and Aaron Brown at CNN—replaced the morning show personalities.

President Bush was in Sarasota, Florida, visiting an elementary school. Moments before he was to make his remarks to the enthusiastic gathering, White House Chief of Staff Andrew Card whispered the news. "Today, we've had a national tragedy," Bush announced. "Two airplanes have crashed into the World Trade Center in an apparent terrorist attack on our country." The president left Florida immediately. Noted Jennings, "The president said the two things which a president must say at a moment like this: terrorism will not stand . . . and God bless the victims and their families." The president's exact whereabouts would be one of the subplots of the day. Without knowing the source or the extent of the attack on America, policy dictated that the president's location be kept secret.

At the same time, air traffic control towers reported that two other airplanes were unaccounted for. Then, thirty-four minutes after the second tower was hit, American Airlines Flight 77 crashed into the Pentagon.

President Bush was headed for Barksdale Air Force

Base in Louisiana. On the way he put the military on high alert and maintained constant contact with Vice President Dick Cheney and other key members of his staff and the government. Bush addressed the American people from the base, making it a point to reassure the citizenry that the full resources of the federal government were working to assist local authorities and to track down the perpetrators.

The rest of the morning became televised chaos, with the networks frantically trying to cover the story. "Television news became a 'community,'" says CNN's Brown. "Everyone across the board understood that this was history. We all shared pictures. None of us thought about competing that day, we just thought about doing this well."

Rumors of other hijacked planes were reported. No one knew exactly what was happening; everything was occurring in real time; and by now everyone was watching. "There were 100 moving parts to the story, in the first three to four hours, particularly," observed Brown. "And I was just trying to make sure that we were right. If we were a little slow on something, that was okay. It was okay to be slow, it was not okay to be wrong."

The panic on the streets of New York was surreal. Reporters on the ground scrambled to tell the story while the emergency crews leaped into action.

Then the towers came down.

At 10 A.M., the South Tower collapsed on live television. Millions of people watched as thousands were buried in the rubble. Twenty-nine minutes later, the North Tower fell. "Good Lord, there are no words," Brown said as he watched along with his audience.

"When the second building went down," Brown recalls, "we all just needed a moment to look at it and think about it. And nothing I could say was going to be as powerful as what viewers saw. Nothing I could add was going to make people feel better or, frankly, worse. It was

Left to right: As the towers crumbled, a dense cloud of smoke and debris sent people fleeing down the streets of lower Manhattan, many covered in ash and dust, barely able to breathe. ■ *White House Chief of Staff Andrew Card informs President Bush about the attack during his visit to a Florida elementary school.* ■ *The New York skyline resembled a war zone.* ■ *Thirty-four minutes later, a third plane crashed into the Pentagon.*

"This is a day when all Americans from all walks of life unite in our resolve for justice and peace."

in New York—redefined American heroism by rushing the hijackers and forcing the plane down. No one knows for certain what target was spared or how many lives on the ground were saved by their selfless act.

Focus turned to the victims, their families, and the heroes who had tried to save them. It was quickly reported that more than 300 New York City police officers, firefighters, and Port Authority workers had lost their lives when the towers collapsed. They had been trying to save those trapped in the buildings. New York Mayor Rudy Giuliani (later named *Time* magazine's Person of the Year) blamed "anger and hatred" for the attack and urged all Americans "to rise above it, as one people, to recover from the tragedy."

As evening fell President Bush arrived back at the White House. Again he addressed the nation and the world on live television. He spoke of terror and its hideous intent. He spoke of evil and America's response to it. He spoke of the

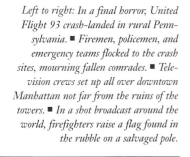

Left to right: In a final horror, United Flight 93 crash-landed in rural Pennsylvania. ▪ Firemen, policemen, and emergency teams flocked to the crash sites, mourning fallen comrades. ▪ Television crews set up all over downtown Manhattan not far from the ruins of the towers. ▪ In a shot broadcast around the world, firefighters raise a flag found in the rubble on a salvaged pole.

all in front of them. I just thought it was a good time to be quiet. It was a country that we all knew in those moments was going to be changed. And to take five seconds or 10 seconds to just let people feel it seemed like the right thing to do."

People were running everywhere and nowhere as a huge cloud of dust and debris filled the corridors of Lower Manhattan. The emotions on the street were fear, terror, and anger. As MSNBC reporter Ashleigh Banfield put it, "This whole place looked like a war zone."

The attacks still weren't over. Six minutes after the first tower collapsed, United Flight 93 crash-landed in rural Pennsylvania, 80 miles from Pittsburgh. It was later learned that a group of passengers—after using cell phones to contact their families and hearing of the attacks

country's strength. He concluded by saying, "This is a day when all Americans from all walks of life unite in our resolve for justice and peace. America has stood down enemies before and we will do so this time. None of us will ever forget this day, yet we go forward to defend freedom and all that is good and just in the world."

Planes crashing, people running, fires burning, buildings collapsing, and spontaneous displays of patriotism—television images engraved forever in the minds of those who watched, images that would band us together to face the consequences of a country transformed by terror. On September 11, 2001, television didn't just tell the story; it became part of the story.

Unforgettable Moments in Television **Sports**

Wide World of Sports

April 29, 1961, to present

It was the summertime fill-in show that became an institution by fulfilling its weekly promise of "Spanning the globe to bring you the constant variety of sport. The thrill of victory and the agony of defeat. The human drama of athletic competition."

Wide World of Sports was the brainchild of Roone Arledge, the programming genius who would turn *Monday Night Football* into a television phenomenon a decade later. Arledge decided that if rivals CBS and NBC had a monopoly on the major sports franchises in America, ABC would focus on other sports around the rest of the world. *Wide World of Sports* carved out its niche in sports television by presenting everything from the Drake Relays in Des Moines to soccer in São Paulo, from chess championships in Reykjavík, Iceland, to table tennis in Tokyo. Along with boxing, drag racing, gymnastics, and ice-skating, *Wide World of Sports* is responsible for some of sports television's most indelible images. Among the most recognizable is the image former *Wide World of Sports* producer Dennis Lewin chose to illustrate "the agony of defeat" in the show's opening sequence.

Left to right: ■ *Ski jumper Vinko Bogataj's crash landing became the opening of the weekly show, highlighting the "agony of defeat."* ■ *Jim McKay announces the World Lumberjack Championships in 1962.* ■ *The Thrilla in Manilla, Ali vs. Frazier.* ■ *Cosell with Ali.*

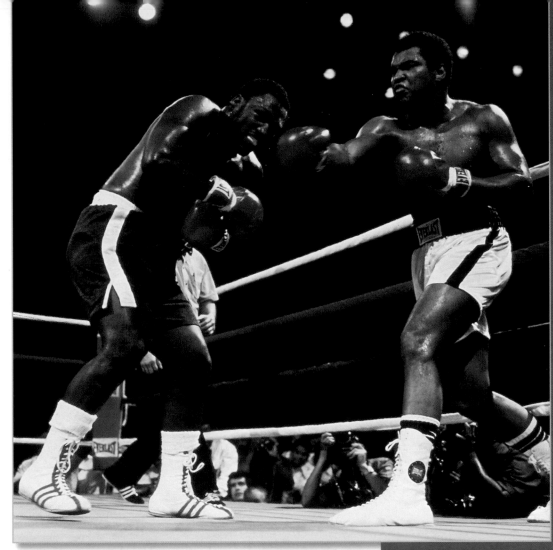

When ski jumper Vinko Bogataj, from the former Yugoslavia, took a run down a ski ramp at the International Ski Flying Championship in Oberstdorf, West Germany, in 1970, he was hoping for a few seconds of exhilaration and a winning leap as he soared through the air. Instead, a camera caught his excruciating plunge into television immortality as he lost his balance and crashed into the snow, skis flying, his body bouncing.

When it turned out Bogataj wasn't seriously hurt, having suffered only a mild concussion, Lewin decided to use his inglorious moment on the opening of their weekly sports spectacle. "I was at a figure skating event in Lubiana, Yugoslavia, watching the ski jumping tournament on Eurovision," explained Lewin. "When I saw Vinko Bogataj take the fall, I told Jim McKay this was going to become the 'agony of defeat' in our show." Lewin had no idea of what it would become.

For *Wide World of Sports*' inaugural show, Roone Arledge planned two live events, a bold venture back in an era before satellite communication became commonplace. The show's host, Jim McKay, would anchor the Penn Relays in Philadelphia while McKay's colleagues Jim Simpson and Bill Flemming would be in Des Moines, Iowa, for the Drake Relays.

Arledge's first major acquisition for *Wide World* was the Amateur Athletic Union events in 1961, including the United States–Soviet Union track meet in Moscow. It was the height of the cold war and athletic competition involving the world's two superpowers often became bigger than the event and an effective way to attract viewers whose patriotic fervor drew them to sports they normally wouldn't watch.

During the first 20 weeks, along with the Moscow track meet, the *Wide World of Sports* schedule included a soccer championship in London, the LeMans auto race from France, and an all-star baseball game in Japan. Rather than a mere summer replacement, *Wide World of Sports* was on its way to a record broadcast run.

While Muhammad Ali gained worldwide fame in the ring and announcer Howard Cosell became synonymous with *Monday Night Football*, their unique relationship is best remembered from their joint appearances on *Wide World of Sports*. Several of Ali's most legendary fights, including bouts

against fellow heavyweight titans Joe Frazier and George Foreman, were first broadcast via closed-circuit pay-per-view in theaters and would replay on *Wide World of Sports* the following Saturday. Ali would join Cosell, offering commentary, hyping his next fight, and playfully sparring with the bombastic broadcaster, threatening to remove the toupee from atop his head.

The Ali-Cosell show within *Wide World of Sports* generated many of the series' most memorable moments. Knowing viewers were hooked on the Ali-Cosell segment, Arledge would schedule it later in the program, forcing his audience to first sit through log rolling or frog jumping or some other quasi sport, thus boosting the ratings for an activity few would normally watch.

"We were pioneering in techniques; we were pioneering in coverage."

Yet for all his popularity, Ali wasn't "the greatest" when it came to *Wide World of Sports* ratings. The ratings champion wasn't even a true athlete. It was stunt performer Evel Knievel, whose daredevil motorcycle jump in King's Mills, Ohio, drew an astonishing 22.3 rating for its 1975 telecast—topping Knievel's previous ratings high for his failed jump attempt at Snake River Canyon in Idaho, in a homemade rocket ship he called the Skycycle. By comparison, replays of Ali's Rumble in the Jungle against George Foreman in Zaire, and his Thrilla in Manila against Joe Frazier in the Philippines achieved 21.7 and 21.0 ratings, respectively.

Seven of the top eight–rated *Wide World of Sports* shows featured either Knievel or Ali; the lone exception was a Harlem Globetrotters game. Producer Dennis Lewin says that it's not surprising so many of the show's higher rated moments revolved around two of the most charismatic individuals of the '70s. "Muhammad Ali was arguably one of the world's greatest figures, not just sports figures. And Evel Knievel struck a chord with people as far as his derring-do. People said Evel was nothing but a huckster, but the reality is Evel put his life on the line, said he was going to do something, and went out and did it."

Although a Knievel appearance could easily become a sideshow, providing fodder for the critics, *World Wide of*

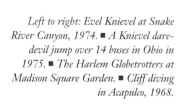

Left to right: Evel Knievel at Snake River Canyon, 1974. ▪ A Knievel daredevil jump over 14 buses in Ohio in 1975. ▪ The Harlem Globetrotters at Madison Square Garden. ▪ Cliff diving in Acapulco, 1968.

Sports kept its overall quality high enough to be critically acclaimed year after year. The show has won 47 Emmys, two Peabody Awards, and numerous other honors.

Arledge's vision of a worldwide format has been realized many times over. "Not only did we look for new events," said Lewin, "but we looked for new ways to do them all the time, and we were pioneering. We were pioneering in techniques; we were pioneering in coverage." *Wide World of Sports* helped develop such techniques as slow motion, overhead cameras, cameras mounted on cranes, and underwater cameras. Methods that are commonplace today were rare in sports television until *Wide World of Sports* began using them on a regular basis.

Now in its fourth decade, *Wide World of Sports* is the longest running sports show in television history and the longest running show of any kind on the ABC network.

Home Run Kings
Maris, McGwire, Bonds

October 1, 1961, September 8, 1998, and October 5, 2001

Since Major League Baseball first appeared on television on August 26, 1939, when fans watched the Brooklyn Dodgers and the Cincinnati Reds split a doubleheader at Ebbets Field over station W2XBS in New York, baseball and television have enjoyed a successful partnership. Television brings fans to the game, and the game, which can turn on every pitch and every at bat, provides dramatic moments for television. Among the most memorable has been the single-season home run derby, the race to capture the most cherished record in all of baseball.

It seemed proper that the New York Yankees' Babe Ruth should hold the single-season home run mark. After all, it was largely Ruth who saved baseball after the Black Sox scandal of 1919, and Ruth who emerged as the most dominant athletic figure of the 1920s, the decade when sports became an American obsession. But by 1961

Right: Fans grab for the record-breaking ball. ▪ Yogi Berra greets Maris at the plate after the record breaker. ▪ Maris wielding the big bat that accounted for 61 home runs in 1961.

Ruth was a legendary figure, known to an entire generation only by grainy black-and-white photos and film footage.

On deck was a challenger, Roger Maris, an upstart Yankee who had never hit more than 39 homers but who now stood poised to break the record of baseball's greatest star and his hallowed single-season home run mark of 60, set in 1927. As the 27-year-old Maris chased Ruth's home run record through July and August and into September, he was subjected to such verbal abuse, even death threats, that anxiety caused chunks of his hair to fall out.

Despite all that Maris kept his concentration on the field, kept his swing pure and, on the final day of the regular season, facing Tracy Stallard of the Boston Red Sox, Maris hit his 61st home run of the season in the fourth inning.

But he was neither lauded nor applauded. A crowd of less than half the capacity showed up that day at Yankee Stadium. The homer was seen locally, but there was no satellite capability to beam the moment live around the nation. Maris achieved his feat and went out for a quiet dinner.

Baseball Commissioner Ford Frick put an asterisk next to the new record because Maris had the advantage of a 162-game schedule—he actually had 163 games because one ended in a rain-caused tie—to break a mark Ruth set in a 154-game season. And, chimed in the critics, Maris had the further advantage of playing in baseball's first expansion season, which watered down the pitching talent.

Ruth had held the record for 34 years. By the time Mark McGwire, playing for the St. Louis Cardinals, began his assault in the 1998 season, Maris's record had stood for 37 seasons.

Like Ruth, McGwire seemed a larger-than-life figure, Superman with a number on his back. Like Ruth, McGwire not only hit home runs but blasted them, producing drives to parts of the ballpark thought to be beyond the reach of flying baseballs. And, like Ruth, McGwire came along at a time when his sport badly needed him. In Ruth's era, baseball was trying to recover from a gambling scandal. In McGwire's time, it was a devastating owners' lockout. So baseball embraced McGwire and celebrated his effort. That effort was made even more memorable by the exuberant presence of Sammy Sosa, the Chicago Cubs slugger. Much as Maris had Mickey Mantle matching him home run for home run through a good deal of the 1961 season, McGwire had Sosa joining him in pursuit of Maris's record.

When that standard fell again on September 8, 1998, there was no dispute. Whereas Maris had needed every game to achieve his accomplishment, McGwire broke the mark in his 145th game. "That was the last night of a home stand," recalls sportscaster Joe Buck, who called the record-breaking home run for the Fox network. "It was against the Cubs. Sosa was in the stadium in right field watching. I interviewed McGwire before the game, and I said, 'What do you think? Is this going to be the night?' And he said, 'This will be the night, I know I'm going to hit it tonight,'" Buck remembers.

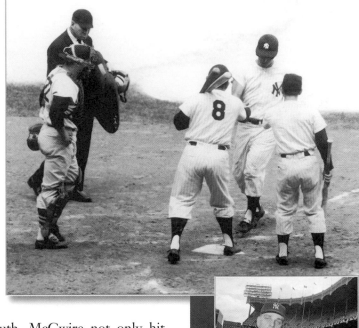

broadcast booth–mates Bob Brenly and Tim McCarver remained silent for more than three and a half minutes as director Bill Webb kept the camera on McGwire, capturing unforgettable images as he rounded the bases, waved to fans, and hugged his teammates and the Maris family.

Finally Buck proclaimed, "Folks, it couldn't happen to a better man, and you will always know where you were at 8:18 P.M. central time, September 8, 1998."

"I think that whole scene after he hit the home run was almost dreamlike," Buck said. "I was looking

Then, at his second at bat, McGwire swung. "Down the left field line, is it enough?" Buck shouted. "Good! There it is, 62!" In all the excitement McGwire nearly missed first base, prompting Buck to comment, "Touch first, Mark." Buck continued, "You're the new single-season home run king!" Fireworks lit up the St. Louis skies. Then Joe Buck and

Left: Busch Stadium in St. Louis as Mark McGwire breaks Maris's record with 62 home runs. ▪ McGwire connects and watches the ball on its way to setting a new record. Right: Celebrating the 62nd home run with teammates. ▪ With Roger Maris's family after breaking the record. ▪ McGwire lifts son Matthew at home plate.

at McGwire lifting up his son. Then, when he went over to the Maris kids to pay tribute to them during his moment, I thought this was the classiest thing I've ever seen on the field."

McGwire went on to dwarf all the sluggers who had gone before him, finishing the season with an incredible 70 home runs. And right behind him was Sosa with 66. Ruth and Maris may have been household names in the baseball world, but with the constant media coverage McGwire and Sosa were on their way to becoming icons.

When Barry Bonds, playing for the San Francisco Giants, began his assault on McGwire's record in 2001, there didn't seem to be much excitement outside his home city. For one thing, the nation was still recovering from the devastating terrorist attacks in New York and Washington, D.C., barely a month earlier. Priorities were altered, and Bonds was not a well-liked figure. He had had rocky relationships with his teammates and with the media. He had been portrayed as self-centered and arrogant. But, like it or not, he was bearing down on McGwire just as resolutely as McGwire had gone after Maris.

On Friday night, October 5, 2001, facing the Giants' hated rivals, the Los Angeles Dodgers, at San Francisco's Pacific Bell Park, Bonds, playing in his 160th game, put McGwire, and everyone else who ever wore a Major League uniform, in his rearview mirror.

While McGwire's record-breaking home run came on a 341-foot fly ball, his shortest home run of the '98 season, Bonds reached his summit in spectacular fashion. Coming up against Dodger right-hander Chan Ho Park in the first

McGwire not only hit home runs but blasted them, producing drives to parts of the ballpark thought to be beyond the reach of flying baseballs.

inning with two out and nobody aboard, Bonds hit a 1–0 fastball at 8:14 P.M. Legendary announcer Jon Miller called it: "There's a high fly deep into right center field! Number 71 and what a shot! Over the 442-foot marker, the deepest part of any ballpark in the National League. And Barry Bonds is now the home run king!" Fans watching on television saw Bonds drop his bat, raise his arms, and circle the bases to the accompaniment of fireworks and a capacity crowd of 41,730 chanting, "Barry! Barry! Barry!" After Bonds coasted around the bases waving to the fans, he was greeted at home plate with hugs from teammates and his family, 11-year-old son Nikolai, 10-year-old daughter Shikari, wife Liz, and mother Pat.

But Bonds wasn't through providing his own fireworks. Up he came again in the third inning. Again Park was on

the mound. The Dodger delivered a 1–1 breaking pitch. The ball screamed into the San Francisco sky, this time toward center field and the 404-foot marker. Again it went out, for Bonds's 72nd home run.

Two days later, on the last day of the regular season, Bonds homered one more time, his 73rd of an unbelievable season. "I've been watching baseball since I was a kid," said Bonds, whose father, Bobby, played in the majors and whose godfather is Willie Mays, "and I've never seen anything like this in my life."

Will anyone ever see it again? Unlike in 1927, 1961, and 1998, nobody is calling Bonds's record out of reach. In this age of sluggers, as home run hitters keep redefining their outer limits, television will be there to capture it.

"I've never seen anything like this in my life."

Left to right: San Francisco Giant Barry Bonds slugs his 71st home run on his way to a new season record. ■ *Bonds hammers the 72nd run, and hugs his 10-year-old son, Nikolai.* ■ *Bonds watches as his 73rd homer flies out of the park.*

Black Power

The Protest at the
1968 Mexico City Games

October 16, 1968

There was much to be remembered and admired about the 1968 U.S. Olympic team in Mexico City. Who could forget the incredible sight of Bob Beamon soaring through the thin air on a long jump for the ages, landing almost two feet beyond the previous world record? Who could forget the joy on the face of George Foreman as he celebrated his gold medal–winning performance in the heavyweight boxing competition by waving an American flag in the ring?

Those were moments made for television.

Yet the lasting television image of those games is neither one of accomplishment nor joy. It was, perhaps, a sporting image that mirrored a year in which ever-growing numbers of Americans rallied in anger and outrage over the devastating losses in Vietnam, the horrifying assassinations of Robert Kennedy and Rev. Dr. Martin Luther King Jr., and the battles in the streets of Chicago between police and protestors at the Democratic National Convention.

Civil rights was a central and volatile issue that year. King's assassination ignited a new round of riots in the minority areas of many American cities that spring. The images of

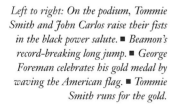

Left to right: On the podium, Tommie Smith and John Carlos raise their fists in the black power salute. ▪ Beamon's record-breaking long jump. ▪ George Foreman celebrates his gold medal by waving the American flag. ▪ Tommie Smith runs for the gold.

the flames that engulfed homes and businesses fanned the unrest and dominated the evening television news.

Even before the 1968 Olympics began, there had been rumors of a boycott by an alliance of black athletes calling themselves the Olympic Project for Human Rights, designed to draw attention to black grievances.

At a New York news conference attended by King, those options were discussed. "It was not a bunch of black athletes wanting to become famous by making trouble or by causing a problem. In fact, we were already famous," said Tommie Smith. Smith held 11 world records at the time and possessed such talent that Lee Evans, gold medalist in the 400 meters in the 1968 Olympics, once said of competing against him, "When Tommie was running fast, he made you lose control of your body."

Ultimately, though, it came down to Smith and John Carlos, who chose to make a political statement on their own.

It happened on October 16 in Mexico City, after Smith won the gold medal in the 200-meter race and Carlos took the bronze. "Oh, my God," Smith thought. "I have done it. Here I am." While in a holding area underneath the stands 20 minutes before the medal ceremony, Smith was sorting through his gym bag and spotted a pair of his black athletic gloves. "I pulled my gloves out of my bag and I looked at them. It came to me then. I knew that I was going to wear the gloves." Smith decided that wearing the black gloves

would add emphasis to his clinched fist in the air. "I wanted to make a point. I wanted to emphasize the fact that what you saw was real." Moments before walking out to the victory ceremony, Smith revealed his plan to his teammate, offering one of the gloves to Carlos.

The two men stood on the victory platform preparing to receive their medals, wearing only black socks on their feet to symbolize black poverty and black scarves around their necks symbolizing their race.

When the medal was put around my neck," said Smith, "that's the first time I noticed the crowd. And that scared me. It seemed like something was just pushing me straight down."

As the band began playing "The Star-Spangled Banner," silver medalist Peter Norman of Australia stood respectfully at attention. Then, in uni-

son, Smith and Carlos raised their clenched fists over their heads and stared at the ground. "It was automatic," Smith said. "It was a prayer of solidarity. The national anthem was being played and I was saying the Lord's Prayer silently."

Olympic officials were infuriated.

At a news conference following the ceremony, Carlos defended their actions. "We want to make it clear that white people seem to think black people are animals doing a job," he said. "We want people to understand that we are not animals or rats. We want you to tell Americans, and all the world, that if they do not care what black people do, they should not go to see black people perform."

> "We want you to tell Americans, and all the world, that if they do not care what black people do, they should not go to see black people perform."

Hit with a wave of outrage, Smith and Carlos were ordered to leave the Olympic Village and found refuge in a small hotel. When ABC sportscaster Howard Cosell found him, Smith told Cosell, as related in the book *Cosell*, "You'd think I committed murder." Smith agreed to an interview. "Are you proud to be an American?" Cosell asked him in front of the cameras. "I am proud to be a black American," Smith replied.

The International Olympic Committee issued a statement saying Smith and Carlos violated Olympic rules "by using the occasion to advertise domestic political views." Douglas F. Roby, president of the United States Olympic Committee, said he asked IOC officials what would happen if the USOC did not discipline Smith and Carlos. According to Roby, he was told the IOC would take "drastic action so far as our team was concerned."

The USOC then expelled Smith and Carlos from the

Left to right: Smith celebrates his victory at the finish line. ■ Smith with fellow medal winner Carlos, their fists rasised in the black power salute as they leave the field.

Games and issued a statement saying the USOC "expresses its profound regrets . . . for the discourtesy displayed by two members of its team in the parting from tradition during the victory ceremony."

There was talk of a walkout by other U.S. athletes to show solidarity with Smith and Carlos, but it never materialized. The anger and outrage over their actions followed them home to the United States.

"You know, as soon as that victory stand was complete, the atrociousness of the system came down upon my family," said Smith. "They began to send cow manure and dead animals to my mother. She died two years later and I think it's because of the stress." One Chicago newspaper referred to Smith and Carlos as "black-skinned storm troopers."

Both men knew in advance their actions would cost them any further chance to run to glory. Smith went on to an unsuccessful tryout with the Cincinnati Bengals as a wide receiver and then turned to coaching. He has been a track coach at Santa Monica College for nearly 25 years.

Carlos, too, attempted to play pro football, but was unsuccessful in tryouts with two teams. He worked for the Los Angeles Olympic Organizing Committee in the 1984 Games but was unemployed for years afterward. Carlos says the 1968 platform demonstration branded him with an unfavorable image he can't shake.

The televised images of Smith and Carlos branded the 1968 Olympics with an image it will never shake.

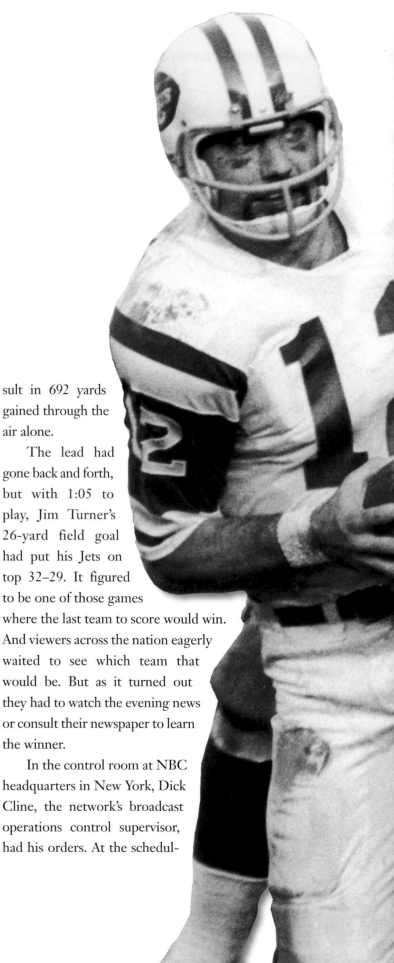

The *Heidi* Game

November 17, 1968

Above: Daryle Lamonica. Far right: The Raiders swarm around Namath.
■ *Namath scores from the one-yard line in the second quarter.*

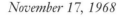

She was just a cute little 10-year-old, prancing across the screen in a made-for-television movie that figured to be soon forgotten. Instead, among football fans, she has been remembered for decades, the mere mention of her name—*Heidi*—stirring up old feelings of anger and outrage. *Heidi* came into America's living rooms on Sunday night, November 17, 1968, on NBC, knocking a pro football game off the air before its climactic moments had been played out. The ensuing uproar ensured that no television executive would ever again question the appeal of pro football on television in prime time.

The game whose end was denied viewers wasn't even an NFL game. It matched the Oakland Raiders and the New York Jets of the old American Football League, condescendingly referred to as the "inferior league" by NFL officials. Not so in the minds of viewers, however. The AFL, trying to lure NFL fans away, was a wide-open, high-scoring league in those days. And nobody could put balls in the air and points on the scoreboard like quarterbacks Joe Namath of the Jets and Daryle Lamonica of the Raiders. That's what Namath and Lamonica were doing that day in a game that would re-

sult in 692 yards gained through the air alone.

The lead had gone back and forth, but with 1:05 to play, Jim Turner's 26-yard field goal had put his Jets on top 32–29. It figured to be one of those games where the last team to score would win. And viewers across the nation eagerly waited to see which team that would be. But as it turned out they had to watch the evening news or consult their newspaper to learn the winner.

In the control room at NBC headquarters in New York, Dick Cline, the network's broadcast operations control supervisor, had his orders. At the schedul-

ing meeting held earlier in the week, NBC's advertising executives announced that Timex had purchased the entire two hours on the network beginning at 7 P.M. eastern standard time to air the movie *Heidi*, the story of a little orphan living with her grandfather in the Swiss Alps. It was an understandable decision at the time. "This was not a concern," Cline says, "because to that point we had never experienced a game going beyond 7 P.M." With the World Series still played in the daytime and *Monday Night Football* two years away from going on the air, the concept of sports in prime time was foreign to TV executives.

Despite their plans, at about 6:30 P.M., Cline became concerned that perhaps, for the first time, the game may run longer than expected. By 6:45 P.M. there was no doubt in Cline's mind that the game was definitely going to last beyond 7 P.M. Cline called his supervisor Scott Connal and the two agreed it would be wise for Connal to contact the network's president, Julian Goodman, to get his permission to stay with the game. Cline waited, but neither Connal nor Goodman phoned with new instructions. Timex was paying good money to advertise on *Heidi*, and calls were beginning to come into the NBC switchboard from viewers concerned whether the movie would be starting on time.

Meanwhile, after the Raiders had returned the kickoff to their own 23-yard line, a 20-yard pass from Lamonica to Charlie Smith became a 35-yard play when the Jets were penalized for grabbing a face mask. That put the ball on the New York 43-yard line with less than a minute to play.

Time for a commercial. Time for a station break. Time for *Heidi*.

"Once we went to the station break, the phone rang," explained Cline. "I answered the phone and it was the presi-

dent of the company." The voice on the other end delivered a terse directive to Cline, "This is Julian Goodman. Go back to the ball game." Although Cline dutifully assured Goodman he would do his best, he knew it was impossible. In the presatellite era of network television, telecasts were carried through a series of prearranged telephone lines. The decision was made earlier in the week to relinquish the line out to the West Coast as soon as the game was finished, or by no later than 7 P.M., whichever came first. When Cline ordered the switch thrown, according to Cline, an "anonymous telephone company engineer somewhere in Iowa," handled the actual switching process.

The volume of protest calls to NBC was instantaneous and so overwhelming that the switchboard blew 26 fuses over the next hour. Even the New York City Police Department received calls from angry Jets fans. It might not have been so bad if the game had ended without another score. Network executives might have placated enraged viewers by telling them they hadn't missed anything. But that was not the case. Lamonica hit Smith on a 43-yard touchdown pass to put Oakland in front 36–32 with 42 seconds to play.

And the Raiders weren't done. Oakland's Preston Ridlehuber recovered a fumble on the ensuing kickoff and scored, giving the Raiders two touchdowns in the final minute after NBC had signed off.

Final score: Oakland 43, New York 32.

The volume of protest calls to NBC was instantaneous and so overwhelming that the switchboard blew 26 fuses over the next hour.

Goodman issued an apology to viewers the same night, calling the incident "a forgivable error committed by humans who were concerned about children expecting to see *Heidi* at 7 P.M. I missed the end of the game as much as anyone else." Syndicated columnist Art Buchwald wrote, "Men who wouldn't get out of their chairs during an earthquake rushed to the phones to scream obscenities." Even newscaster David Brinkley chimed in, blaming the move on "the faceless button pusher in the bowels of NBC," and then replayed the crucial final minute of the game on *The Huntley-Brinkley Report*.

The Jets went on that season to beat the Baltimore Colts in Super Bowl III, a monumental upset that garnered huge ratings and further promoted the merger of the NFL and the AFL.

As a result of the *Heidi* debacle, NFL television contracts now guarantee that games of visiting clubs must air in their home markets in their entirety. Pro football became a ratings monster, devouring everything counterprogrammed against it.

Poor *Heidi* never had a chance.

Left to right: Smith scores in the third quarter. ▪ Sir Michael Redgrave and Jennifer Edwards in Heidi. *▪ Davidson zeroes in on Namath. ▪ Turner's field goal put the Jets ahead with 65 seconds to play. ▪ Smith scores to put Oakland ahead with 42 seconds left in the game.*

Monday Night Football

September 21, 1970, to present

In 1970, before football became a fixture in prime time and Super Bowls routinely scored record-setting ratings, the idea of networks staging an NFL game on a Monday night was considered foolish for even the most desperate prime-time schedules. CBS had already tried prime-time games twice, even featuring the highly popular Green Bay Packers, led by Vince Lombardi, but the experiment had not been a ratings success. Conventional wisdom suggested that women controlled television at night, and women did not like football.

But none of this discouraged NFL Commissioner Pete Rozelle. In the years since *Monday Night Football* soared into the elite list of top shows, many names have been linked to its success. But it was Rozelle who conceived the idea and Rozelle who sold it to ABC, a network desperately wanting to break the stranglehold of its two competitors, CBS and NBC, in prime time.

While Rozelle may have conceived the idea of the NFL in prime time, Roone Arledge, then the president of ABC Sports, knew how to execute it. Arledge knew ABC couldn't just do Sunday afternoon football on Monday night. If his

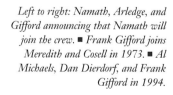

Left to right: Namath, Arledge, and Gifford announcing that Namath will join the crew. ■ Frank Gifford joins Meredith and Cosell in 1973. ■ Al Michaels, Dan Dierdorf, and Frank Gifford in 1994.

sportscast was going to compete with entertainment programming, he had to stress entertainment over athletics. Dennis Lewin, the original producer of *Monday Night Football*, recalls, "CBS and NBC had actually passed on the opportunity to do *Monday Night Football*, because they felt (a) it would never work in prime time and (b) their Monday night lineup was too strong. So it was Roone who was the visionary to do it in a form that wasn't just X's and O's. It was a form that would appeal to an entertainment audience, not just a sports audience."

Arledge's concept started in the broadcast booth. He felt he could combine the best elements of sports and entertainment by forming a team that could emulate Rowan and Martin for laughs, Huntley and Brinkley for incisive reporting, and maybe even Lucy and Ricky for ridiculous behavior. He paired Keith Jackson, one of the best play-by-play men in the business, with two very different personalities, the urbane, tell-it-like-it-is, hard-driving editorial voice of Howard Cosell and the fun-lovin' Texan, former Dallas Cowboys quarterback Don Meredith. "The three created, for want of a better phrase, 'watercooler' talk," says Lewin. "Every Tuesday morning people all over the country would say, 'Hey, did you hear what Howard said to Don, or what Don said to Howard, what was said about this coach, what was said about that player?' It created a whole different atmosphere."

Monday Night Football debuted on September 21, 1970, in Cleveland, with the Browns

tweak Howard, and Meredith also knew how to appeal to the average fan. And, you know, the two of them playing off each other—Howard in his erudite way and Meredith in his corn-pone way, both of them extremely intelligent, both of them playing it for everything it was worth, and both knowing exactly what they were doing—were an incredible team." America either loved Cosell or loved to see him shot down. Whichever their attitude, viewers watched in huge numbers.

Even Cosell's masterful halftime narration highlights from the Sunday games, done totally extemporaneously in one take, became controversial. Cosell wasn't the one who picked the games shown. Yet he was on the receiving end of abuse from furious fans in cities that were left out.

In addition to the three-man broadcast booth, ABC outdid its Sunday competitors from a technical standpoint. While most Sunday games in the 1970s employed four or five cameras, *Monday Night Football* used nine, including a sideline camera and two handhelds. But the early reviews were harsh. Despite all

America either loved Cosell or loved to see him shot down. Whichever their attitude, viewers watched in huge numbers.

against the New York Jets. The chemistry was magical. Cosell would deliver what he considered the final word on the state of the game, the state of the league and, often, the state of the union. He used his mastery of the language to articulate his views and his unique staccato cadence to rivet attention, although his eloquence often lapsed into bombast.

"Cosell brought a dynamic personality with a sense of journalism," says Lewin. "He wasn't afraid to take on subjects and offend people. He knew how to evoke emotions not only out of the people around him but the people listening to him." Of the bantering between Cosell and Meredith, Lewin says, "Meredith knew how to

the innovation and theatrics, television critics predicted *Monday Night Football* would achieve no more than a 24 percent share of the audience. Nevertheless, the show got a 31 share in its first season and an impressive 18.5 rating.

After that season Arledge felt the need to bring in one more big name. Jackson was switched to college football, where he has become the sport's dominating figure in the broadcast booth. Replacing him was former NFL great Frank Gifford, who came over from CBS. Gifford settled in and remained a staple in the booth for nearly 30 years. "Nothing was ever said to us in terms of how we were going to do the broadcast, what kind of a role each would play. I think it was a reflection of each of our personalities," he explains. "I had no ego problem with letting Howard and Don become the stars of the show. I wanted to do the best football I could do under sometimes adverse conditions, depending upon the mood of the night. It surprised even us, just how big it grew."

Monday Night Football changed not only the face of prime time but also America's Monday night habits. Restaurants and sports bars drew big crowds by staging *Monday Night Football* parties. Tossing a brick through a television set when Cosell's face appeared became a popular contest. It wasn't unusual for politicians, musicians, and movie stars—from Richard Nixon and Ronald Reagan to John Lennon and John Wayne—to show up in the broadcast booth. The rival networks, which had once laughed at the concept of football in prime time, scampered to find effective counterprogramming.

Cosell left *Monday Night Football* after the 1983 season. Meredith left in 1984. Over the years former players Fred Williamson, Alex Karras, Fran Tarkenton, O. J. Simpson, Joe Namath, Dan Dierdorf, and Boomer Esiason have also sat in the *Monday Night Football* broadcast booth. Al Michaels has been the play-by-play voice since 1986. In the year 2000, seeking to invigorate a show heading into its fourth decade, ABC added comedian Dennis Miller, along with Hall of Fame quarterback Dan Fouts, to the broadcast crew. The use of Miller drew criticism along with praise, generating a kind of controversy not heard since Cosell's time.

For the start of the 2002–03 season the team in the broadcast booth was pared down to just two. Former NFL coach and veteran broadcaster John Madden joined Michaels on Monday nights. There are no complaints at ABC. *Monday Night Football* is the longest running and most successful prime-time sports series in television history, an ongoing phenomenon.

Left to right: The fans loved to hate Cosell. ■ New York Jets vs. Detroit in 1982. ■ Cosell and Gifford in 1981. ■ San Diego vs. Oakland, 1981. ■ Al Michaels with John Madden.

1972 Munich Olympics Crisis

September 5, 1972

At the 1972 Olympic Games in Munich, West Germany, the manufactured life-and-death urgency of athletic competition was brutally jarred into reality by a true life-and-death situation, and television abruptly shifted its gaze from scenes of triumph to scenes of terror.

In the early morning hours of September 5, 1972, the pageantry and drama of the Olympic Games was assailed when the violence and drama of the Middle East conflict unexpectedly played out in the Olympic Village. Eight armed terrorists, calling themselves the Black September organization, evaded Olympic security to break into two apartments housing members of the Israeli team. Two Israelis were killed and two others escaped, leaving nine hostages.

The terrorists demanded the release of more than 200 Arab prisoners being held in Israeli jails. In addition, they wanted safe passage for themselves and their captives out of Germany, and if their demands were not met they threatened to kill the Israeli athletes one by one.

ABC Sports had the telecast rights to the Munich Games. Under the command of executive producer Roone Arledge, director Don Ohlmeyer, and anchor Jim McKay, the network immediately dedicated all its available resources to coverage of the standoff. "In 1972, quite frankly, the news department wasn't well equipped to come on the air with the story," says former ABC Sports producer Dennis Lewin. "We already had cameras everywhere."

Since security had closed off all avenues where the hostages were being held, members of the media were left

Left to right: A terrorist peers from a balcony at the Olympic Village. ■ Anchor Jim McKay and ABC Sports dedicated every available resource to reporting the crisis. ■ Satellite broadcasts beamed live pictures of the apartments under siege. ■ The ABC control room. ■ Police move in on the terrorists.

to their own devices to cover the story. ABC's Middle East correspondent Peter Jennings was on hand, and he and a producer managed to slip into the Olympic Village before security personnel sealed it off. Jennings snuck into the building housing Italian athletes and made it to a window on an upper floor. He had an excellent view from which to report on the negotiations between the terrorists and German officials. So determined was Jennings to remain on the scene that when security men evacuated the building, he hid in a bathroom.

ABC sportscaster Howard Cosell and *Sports Illustrated* photographer Tony Triolo gained access by convincing a guard they were shoe salesmen. Bill Toomey, who had won the decathlon in the 1968 Olympic Games and was an ABC commentator at Munich, put on athletic gear and jogged past guards into the Olympic Village without so much as a second look.

ABC kept their cameras trained on the apartment where the hostages and their captors were holed up, occasionally catching a glimpse of one of the masked, gun-toting terrorists peering from the balcony. McKay and Jennings served as the eyes and ears of America throughout that agonizing day.

Despite mounting criticism, Olympic officials continued competition until around 4 P.M., when they suspended the Games. Deadlines passed into new deadlines, day turned into night and, at last, stalemate turned into an agreement. The terrorists and their hostages would be

taken by helicopter to a nearby airfield where a plane was waiting to fly them, as demanded, to Cairo.

When the group arrived at Fürstenfeldbruck airport, the West German police launched an ambush that ended tragically, with all nine hostages killed. Five died when a

"Our worst fears have been realized tonight. They're all gone."

terrorist threw a grenade into their helicopter. The other four were gunned down. The first report to a waiting world was that the hostages had all survived the ordeal. It was left to ABC's Jim McKay to reveal the horrible truth.

While the gun battle raged at the airport, McKay, Jennings, and ABC Sports commentator Chris Schenkel continued to report the news as it was being relayed to them. Lewin recalls, "Not only was Jim carrying the ball that day in describing these events to the American public, he felt a great sense of burden not to report anything unless it was well documented. He knew there were people watching at home that were going to get all their information from him, and he didn't want to pass along anything that was hearsay. He knew at least one of the Israelis had American parents, and they'd be watching his account of the story."

Finally, McKay, visibly shaken by the information he'd just received in his earpiece from Arledge in the control room, announced, "Our worst fears have been realized tonight. They're all gone."

"I think Jim summed up everybody's mood," says Lewin. "I think everybody was stunned, everybody was shocked. This wasn't supposed to happen at a sporting event. It wasn't supposed to happen period. But, by the same token, I think ABC Sports conducted themselves in an incredibly professional way, led by Roone Arledge and Jim McKay."

On the afternoon of the next day, following a memorial service for the slain athletes, the Games resumed. Allowing the Games to continue outraged many who felt International Olympic Committee president Avery Brundage had not shown the proper respect. Wrote columnist Jim Murray in the *Los Angeles Times*, "Incredibly, they're going on with it. It's almost like having a dance at Dachau."

The tragedy of the Munich Games left an indelible tableau in the minds of the millions who watched, and it reshaped both the world of sports and the world around it for decades to come.

Left to right: The terrorists negotiate with West German officials. ▪ A German army bus carries the terrorists and the hostages to the helicopter pad at the Olympic Village. ▪ Flags at half staff behind the Olympic Torch. ▪ Grieving athletes from Israel and around the world mourned the senseless slaughter.

The Battle of the Sexes

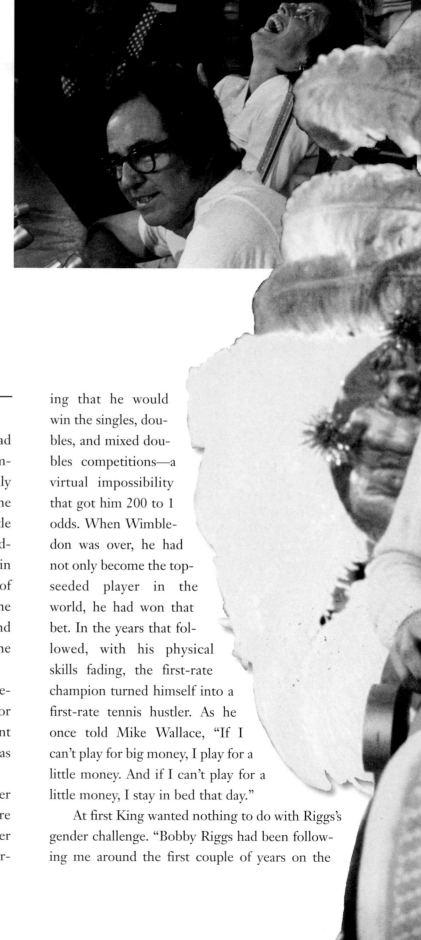

September 20, 1973

I t was a spectacle unlike anything the tennis world had witnessed before. Oddly enough, it wasn't for a championship or a title, and the challengers weren't equally matched. It wasn't even the six-figure purse that coaxed the current reigning women's champion to the court to battle the aging former men's champion and undisputed world-class hustler. Ultimately it was about bragging rights. Yet in the bra-burning era of the women's liberation movement of the 1970s, it was a match of great significance, bringing the nation's attention to the inequities between men's and women's professional sports while truly demonstrating the power of television.

The female gender could not have been better represented. Wimbledon champion Billie Jean King was a major force in the women's professional sports empowerment movement of the early 1970s and, at 29 years old, she was in her athletic prime.

In 1939, five years before King was even born, her opponent Bobby Riggs played at Wimbledon's Centre Court for the first time. He also began his hustling career that same year. Riggs placed a sizable bet on himself, wagering that he would win the singles, doubles, and mixed doubles competitions—a virtual impossibility that got him 200 to 1 odds. When Wimbledon was over, he had not only become the top-seeded player in the world, he had won that bet. In the years that followed, with his physical skills fading, the first-rate champion turned himself into a first-rate tennis hustler. As he once told Mike Wallace, "If I can't play for big money, I play for a little money. And if I can't play for a little money, I stay in bed that day."

At first King wanted nothing to do with Riggs's gender challenge. "Bobby Riggs had been following me around the first couple of years on the

Top: Riggs amuses King at a prematch news conference. Right: Riggs makes a grand entrance, then presents King with a Sugar Daddy sucker before the match.

Slims tour, and he kept saying, 'Billie you got to play this match,' and I said, 'Bobby, stop right there, I am not going to play you. Right now the Virginia Slims tour is the most important thing in my life, and I've got to put my heart and soul into it.' And he goes, 'Oh we got to play and we can make lots of money,' and I go, 'Bobby, I'm not going to play you.'"

Undaunted by King's rebuff, Riggs managed to coerce Australian tennis champion Margaret Smith Court. When he beat her in straight sets, the press dubbed the match the Mother's Day massacre, and King was livid. "Margaret didn't feel that she was playing for anyone but herself, and I was personally upset," recalls King. "It was a put-down, and I didn't like that. It wasn't about tennis, it was about social change, and I knew that going in." Now Riggs would get his match with King, and the Battle of the Sexes was on.

The match, which also became known as the Libber versus the Lobber, was promoted by Jerry Perenchio, who promoted the first Muhammad Ali–Joe Frazier superfight, and it was hyped to the hilt. The ABC television network won the bidding war to broadcast the event, reportedly paying $750,000, and the match was shown via satellite to 36 countries. Football and announcing great Frank Gifford, who did interviews for the ABC telecast, remembers the match started out as a joke and, because of the hype, "It . . . became the hottest ticket of the year, I guess, in sports. . . . All of a sudden . . . the whole country was focused on this match."

Johnson, Jim Brown, and George Foreman. And an estimated 50 million more watched on television.

ABC brought in legendary sportscaster Howard Cosell to host their telecast and added women's tennis pro Rosie Casals, a last-minute replacement made at King's insistence to "balance" the reporting, as his cohost.

Interviewed beforehand by Gifford, and in typical bombastic fashion, Riggs declared the event "the greatest match in tennis history" and asserted that "the male is King, the male is Supreme." Asked about her view of feminism, King took a measured stance. "The women's movement is important to me, as long as it stays practical. And I

"It was a put-down and I didn't like that. It wasn't about tennis, it was about social change, and I knew that going in."

Left: King played hard and won the match in straight sets. Right: King proudly displays her trophy. ■ *At a post-match news conference, the two showed there were no hard feelings.*

By the time the match began, the stakes had increased to nearly $200,000 for the winner and $100,000 for the loser. Add in the endorsements and commercial deals, and the payday for the battling racket-eers was much higher. A spokesman for Riggs claimed that his boss took home over $1 million for his day's work. The event was staged at the Houston Astrodome in front of more than 30,000 people, the largest paid attendance in tennis history. Tickets were priced at a staggering $100 a seat, even more for scalped ones. Courtside seats were studded with celebrities of the day like Andy Williams, George Plimpton, Oleg Cassini, Glen Campbell, and Blythe Danner; and sports stars like Rosie Grier, Rafer

championship fight. Despite the prematch hoopla, there was only one moment when the outcome was in doubt. In the fifth game of the first set, Riggs broke King's serve to take a 3–2 lead. If he held serve, he would take a 4–2 lead and be in control of the set. But King broke back to tie the match at 3–3. She took three of the next four games to win the first set 6–4, as Riggs double-faulted on set point.

Riggs's strategy was to bamboozle his opponent with his array of dinks, lobs, and spins, a plan that kept him in the match for a while. King's strategy was elemental but extremely effective—she simply ran Riggs all over the court. As his body began wearing out, he gave up on shots he had chased down earlier, and King won the second set 6–3. In the third set, Riggs suffered hand cramps and rubbery legs, and King rolled over him 6–3.

As a true sporting event, the Battle of the Sexes was essentially meaningless. But it did prove that there was a huge untapped audience for women's tennis. "It grew beyond either one of their dreams," says Gifford. "But I think it affected Billie Jean King more than it did Bobby Riggs because she sort of had the burden of all the women in the world on her shoulders."

think the women's movement is really making a better life for a lot of people, other than just women."

The extravaganza began with each of the contenders entering the arena in flamboyant fashion. King was brought out on an Egyptian litter adorned with a large Mardi Gras–style feathered appendage, carried on the shoulders of a team of musclemen. Riggs's rickshaw-style cart was attended by a complement of female models, appropriately named Bobby's Bosom Buddies. At a pre-match courtside ceremony, Riggs presented King with a huge Sugar Daddy sucker, and King reciprocated by giving her self-described male chauvinist opponent a real live pig she named Larimore Hustle.

The large, boisterous crowd cheered on both players in a circuslike atmosphere resembling that of a heavyweight

The Perfect 10s
Comaneci and Retton

Nadia Comaneci captivated an international audience with her dynamic gymnastics performance in 1976. Lower right: Comaneci stands before the scoreboard that had to post her perfect 10 as 1.00.

July 18, 1976, and August 3, 1984

Television networks ardently compete for the right to broadcast the Olympics and spend billions of dollars presenting the pageantry and hoping for drama that will attract viewers and generate even more in advertising revenues. At the Montreal Games in 1976, and again at the 1984 Games in Los Angeles, the ABC network and its viewers got more than they had hoped for; they got perfection.

In most sports, perfection is in the eye of the beholder. But in gymnastics, it is easily definable. Perfection is a score of 10. That score had never been posted in Olympic competition heading into the 1976 Games. But that year a four-foot, 11-inch, 86-pound dynamo from Romania named Nadia Comaneci achieved the seemingly unreachable mark.

Comaneci wasn't the favorite in the individual events when the competition began. That role belonged to Russia's Olga Korbut, the reigning gold medalist from the 1972

Olympics. But Comaneci quickly became the favorite of the crowd on July 18, 1976, with her performance on the uneven bars, the first compulsory exercise. She was hoping for a 9.9. But ABC commentator Cathy Rigby, on hand that day at the Montreal Forum, had no doubt what the judges' scores would be. "The only thing people could do at that point was give her a 10," said Rigby, herself a gymnast in both the 1968 and 1972 Games, and the first American woman to win a medal in world gymnastics competition. "Because she was that much better than everybody else. . . . She was really perfect, absolutely perfect. . . . It wasn't even about reading people's minds. It was just, you knew it."

Sure enough, Comaneci got her 10. Yet the Montreal officials were so unprepared for the possibility of a 10 that the scoreboard was programmed to go only as high as 9.99. Comaneci's 10 was posted as 1.00.

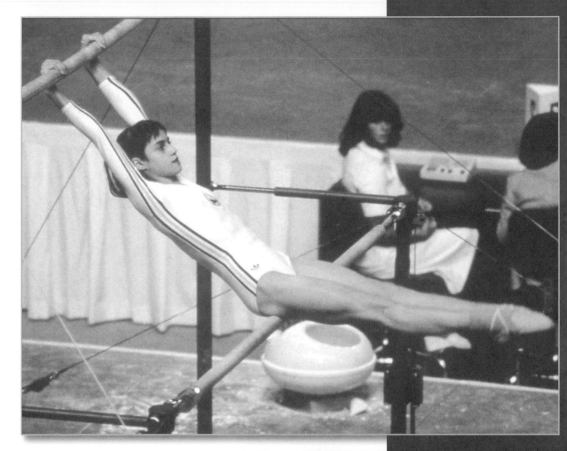

Rigby had first seen the Romanian a year earlier at the European championships, where the commentator already sensed greatness. "She was just this little kind of perky [person], almost the devil-may-care attitude," Rigby said. "Even back then . . . you thought, This person is going to do amazing things. She just had no fear. You never sensed that she was going to make a mistake, even then."

By the time the 1976 Olympic competition was over, Comaneci had collected seven scores of 10, three gold medals, two silvers, and a bronze. "And every little girl wanted to put her hair in pigtails and tumble and jump and play on the uneven bars," said Rigby. "Television provided amazing exposure. It put a face on gymnastics, and gyms filled up with little kids wanting to do this."

Eight years later Rigby was behind the ABC network microphone when perfection appeared again on the Olympic stage. This time, it was an American achieving the ultimate honor on her native soil. Mary Lou Retton of

Fairmont, West Virginia, was still an extreme long shot going into the final two events of the women's individual all-around gymnastics competition at the 1984 Games in Los Angeles. In order to wrest the gold from a pair of Romanians—Ecaterina Szabo and Simona Pauca—Retton would need a perfect score in both events. Even history was against her. No U.S. women's gymnast had ever won a single individual medal of any color.

While Rigby had had ultimate faith in Comaneci, she wasn't so sure about the unheralded Retton. "You were a little bit on edge about it," she said. "So that added to the cliff-hanger. Will she? Is this going to work out? . . . That made

it more exciting at the end." Rigby never doubted, however, that Retton would be a factor. "Even though she was teeny-weeny," said Rigby of the four-foot, nine-inch Retton, "she was just a little powerhouse of an athlete."

As an eight-year-old, Retton had sat transfixed in front a television and watched Comaneci scale the Olympian heights to perfection. Now she was about to attempt the same daunting climb.

On August 3, 1984, it came down to the vault, her best event. As Retton prepared for the greatest moment of her athletic career, Szabo finished up on the uneven bars with a 9.9. Then Retton knew for sure. She would need a 9.95 to

Retton . . . concluded by hitting the mat squarely, arms raised, chest thrown out, as if defying the judges to give her anything but a 10.

Above: Former champion gymnast Cathy Rigby announced Comaneci's victory in 1976, as well as Mary Lou Retton's perfect scores in 1984. Far right: Retton celebrates her four perfect 10s.

tie for the gold medal, a 10 to win. "Now or never," her coach, Bela Karolyi, told her.

It was now. Retton, her pixie smile lighting up UCLA's Pauley Pavilion, concluded by hitting the mat squarely, arms raised, chest thrown out, as if defying the judges to give her anything but a 10. Again, Rigby didn't need the judges' scorecards to rate what she had just seen. "She landed and put her hands up, and everybody just knew," she said. "There was no room for the judge to go, 'Well, I think maybe she was a little low on this part, a little high on this part. . . . There was nothing they could take off."

One after another, four 10s were posted. Retton had

beaten Szabo for the gold by 5/100ths of a point, Pauca by half a point.

The crowd of 9,023 erupted. The chants of "Mary Lou! Mary Lou!" emanated from every corner of the arena. U.S. flags seemed to be in every hand, saluting America's newest sweetheart. Like Comaneci before her, Retton soaked in the glory of a perfect day, and once again television coverage gave gymnastics a name and a face.

Lake Placid 1980

"Do You Believe in Miracles?"

February 22, 1980

When the U.S. Olympic hockey team faced-off against the Soviet squad on the evening of February 22, 1980, at Lake Placid, New York, the clash was a tailor-made television drama. The Soviets were heavily favored while the U.S. team was a decided underdog. And relations between these bitter cold war rivals had grown even icier after President Jimmy Carter's threat to boycott the upcoming Summer Olympic Games in Moscow in retaliation for the Soviet Union's invasion of Afghanistan two months earlier. National pride and politics permeated the arena. For the players and those watching, it was more than a game. It was us against them. David versus Goliath. World War III fought on an ice hockey rink.

From 1956 through 1976, the Soviet

Top left: Steve Christoff attacks the Soviet goal in the first period of the playoff. Bottom left: Mark Johnson prepares to shoot the second U.S. goal. Far right: The American hockey team in action (top). ▪ Smashing collisions with the boards were typical for both sides in the bruising play of the game.

team dominated Olympic play. The U.S.S.R. had won the gold medal at four of the previous five Winter Games, compiling a remarkable 33–3–2 record. The Soviets were a tight-knit, veteran unit and many of the players had competed in previous Olympics. Many of their stars—including goaltender Vladislav Tretiak, defenseman Viacheslav Fetisov, and captain Boris Mikhailov—were considered among the best players in the world.

The last time the U.S. team had won Olympic gold was in 1960 at the Squaw Valley Games. Twelve years later the U.S. won the silver medal at the 1972 Winter Olympics in Sapporo, Japan.

The 1980 U.S. team was composed of college students and semiprofessionals lacking both Olympic experience and a winning tradition. Coach Herb Brooks did have Olympic experience, though; he had played on the 1964 and 1968 U.S. squads and had been the last player cut from the 1960 team. As head coach at the University of Minnesota, he'd guided the Gophers to three national titles in the 1970s, and with his rigorous coaching style, he had earned a reputation as a disciplinarian.

At the tryout camp in Colorado Springs in August 1979, 68 players vied for spots on the team. Brooks selected 26. Before the Games, he whittled the team down to 20 players who came from colleges across the United States: Goalie Jim Craig, forward Dave Silk, and captain Mike Eruzione went to Boston University. Star center Mark Johnson attended the University of Wisconsin. Nine of them had played for

Brooks at the University of Minnesota. The average age of the team was 22 years old.

Brooks devised a simple but radical plan. Instead of playing "NHL-style" hockey, with an emphasis on fighting and checking, he instilled an "international" style, emphasizing weaving and passing. He also stressed conditioning, making his players do endless wind sprints they contemptuously dubbed "Herbies." He told his players, "Gentlemen, you don't have enough talent to win on talent alone."

Brooks used the next six months to mold his players into a cohesive unit. Before the Olympics, they played 61 games, compiling a 42–16–3 record. They showed progress—winning the Lake Placid Invitational in December by beating Sweden, Canada, Czechoslovakia, and the Russian "B" squad. But three days before the Olympics, they were soundly whipped by the Soviets, 10–3, at an exhibition game at Madison Square Garden.

ABC sportscaster Al Michaels, who would be doing the play-by-play for the Olympic hockey telecasts, was at the Garden that night. "The score might as well have been twenty to one," he recalls. "But that's how dominant the Soviets were in almost every game they had played leading up to the Olympics. They never eked out a victory. You never had the feeling they were going to lose."

At Lake Placid, the Americans were seeded seventh out of eight teams. They opened the tournament against Sweden, the number three seed. Trailing 2–1 late in the third period, Brooks pulled goalie Craig for a 6–5 skating advantage. Bill Baker scored the tying goal with less than a minute remaining as the U.S. escaped with a 2–2 draw. Two days later, the U.S. trounced Czechoslovakia 7–3, a major confidence booster, considering that the Czechs were the 1976 Olympic silver medalists. Behind Craig's excellent play in net, the U.S. reeled off three consecutive wins, beating Norway 5–1, Romania 7–2, and West Germany 4–2.

The last victory propelled the U.S. into the medal round, along with the U.S.S.R., Finland, and Sweden. The U.S. team would face the Soviets first, who had cruised through the tournament undefeated at 5–0, with 51 goals scored and only 11 goals against.

The U.S. team and the Soviets met at the Lake Placid Olympic Ice Center on Friday, February 22. Center-ice tickets priced at $67.20 were going for over $300.

Because the face-off occurred at 5:30 P.M. on the East Coast, the game was not broadcast live. Instead, the ABC television network aired it on tape-delay during prime time, with broadcaster Al Michaels and former Montreal Canadiens and Hall of Fame goalie Ken Dryden doing the play-by-play.

Before the game started, Michaels discussed with Dryden his concerns that it not become a repeat of the Madison Square Garden trouncing. "The conversation was something along the lines of, you know, if this can be a two-goal game midway through the second period, if the Soviets only lead three to one, or two to nothing, that might be as good as it gets in terms of keeping the audience interested in the game."

Before the U.S. team took to the ice, the normally taciturn Brooks gave the players a rousing pep talk. "You're meant to be here," he told them. "This moment is yours."

In their trademark red jerseys, the Soviets scored first and held a 2–1 lead late in the first period. But with one second remaining in the period, Mark Johnson scored off an errantly played rebound to even the contest. Furious, Soviet coach Viktor Tikhonov pulled the legendary Tretiak in favor of backup goalie Vladimir Myshkin for the remainder of the game.

In the second period, the Soviets again took the lead. But Jim Craig kept the Americans in the match. Though the Soviets had outshot the U.S. 30 to 10, they led only 3–2.

Midway through the third period, Johnson scored again, tying the game. Less than two minutes later, captain Eruzione sent a wrist shot past Myshkin, sending the roaring, standing-room-only crowd of 8,000 into delirium, chanting, "U.S.A.! U.S.A.!"

"When Eruzione scored, the place was just going crazy," recalls Michaels. "The Soviets seemed to be out of rhythm." Michaels also remembers the elation was palpable. "The building is shaking. It's just rocking like no arena I've ever been in in my life. The sound level is off the charts. When it gets loud enough, sound has feel. I remember feeling the sound over the last minute of that game."

The Russians swarmed Craig for the remainder of the game, but he held fast. Michaels described the action as the excitement mounted and the final seconds ticked away. "Eleven seconds, you got ten seconds, the countdown going on right now. Morrow up to Silk! The crowd taking up the countdown. . . . Five seconds left on the clock!"

"All of a sudden, I looked at the clock and there was no time for the Soviets to score," Michaels remembers. "So that afforded me the opportunity to say something at the end of the game. And the word that came into my head at that point was *miraculous*. Somehow *miraculous* becomes part of a question. Do you believe in miracles?"

As time expired, Michaels permanently etched the improbable triumph into the imaginations of all who watched as he shouted, "Do you believe in miracles?"

"YES!" he answered at the buzzer.

The players hugged each other, their sticks and an American flag raised to the air, creating one of the most poignant and lasting images in the history of sports television. The apprehension and doubt leading up to the contest gave way to feelings of sheer joy, exuberance, and pride. The victory transcended sports. The decibel level in the arena was nearly deafening as the crowd stood cheering. Final score: 4–3, U.S., in one of the greatest upsets in Olympic history.

"When it gets loud enough, sound has feel. I remember feeling the sound over the last minute of that game."

The victory over the Soviets did not clinch the gold medal for the United States. Two days later, the team played Finland. If the Americans lost that game, they would receive a bronze medal, with the gold going to the Soviets.

Finland scored first—the sixth time in seven games that the U.S. surrendered the initial score—and they led 2–1 after two periods. Showing the heart of a champion, the U.S. refused to fold. Early in the third period, Dave Christian (whose father had played on the 1960 team) assisted on a goal by Phil Verchota to tie the score. Minutes later, Rob McClanahan scored to give the U.S. the lead. An insurance goal scored shorthanded by Johnson made the final tally 4–2. The gold medal was theirs. The Soviets took the silver and Sweden the bronze.

Surveying the action again from the broadcast booth, Michaels exclaimed, "The impossible dream comes true!"

At the medal ceremony, captain Mike Eruzione mounted the podium alone. After the playing of "The Star-Spangled Banner," he motioned for his teammates to join him. The Lake Placid crowd roared its approval. The Boys of Winter had done it.

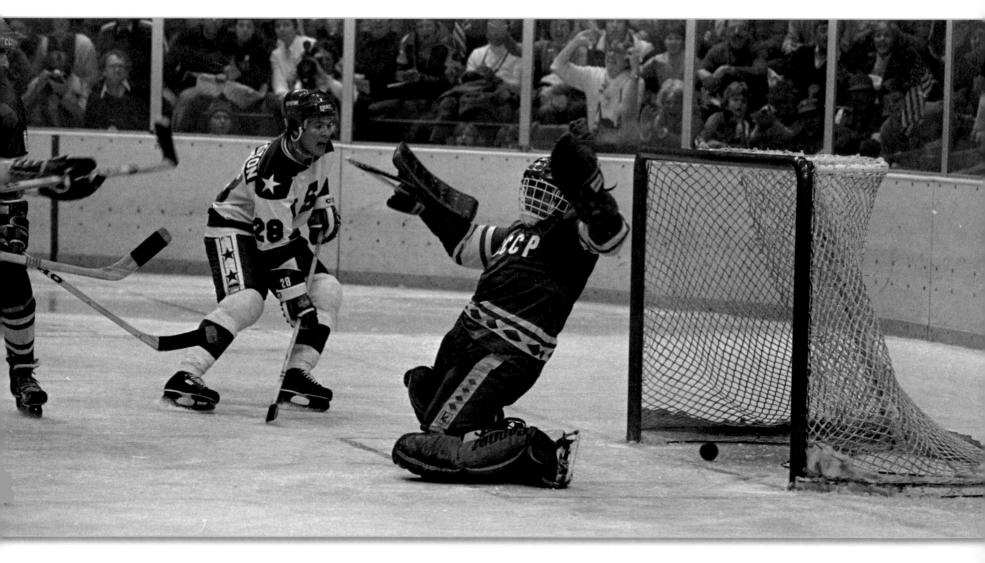

Left: The winning goal from another angle. Right: American team members mobbed each other jubilantly on the ice, and later joined Eruzione on the medal podium.

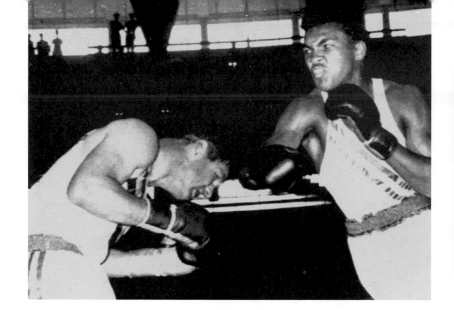

Ali Lights the Centennial Torch

July 19, 1996

Left to right: Ali fighting for the gold in 1960. ■ The opening ceremony at the Olympic Stadium in Atlanta.

More than the pageantry of the parade of nations, more than the elaborate production numbers with lavishly costumed casts of thousands, more than the superstar performances or magnificent pyrotechnic spectacles, in the entire multimillion-dollar extravaganza that is the Olympic opening ceremony, nothing compares to the excitement of the lighting of the Olympic flame. It's the crescendo, the "Christmas morning" of the ceremony. And in 1996 it was the combination of that highly emotional moment and the presence of one of the world's most renowned figures that indelibly etched the event into Olympic television history.

The Olympic flame endures as the Games' most hallowed symbol. In the ancient Games, held in Olympia, Greece, the sacred flame burned on an altar to honor the goddess Hera. The Olympic flame first reappeared in 1928, at the Amsterdam Summer Games. The Berlin Games of 1936 saw the return of another ancient custom, the torch relay. Beginning with a ceremony in Greece, the flame was passed from runner to runner until it arrived in Berlin. For the host country and city, the relay of the flame to the open-

ing ceremony has become an integral part of rousing interest in the Games. Since the dawn of the television age, *who* lights the Olympic flame has become as important as *how* it is lit.

Broadcasting the Olympics is a high-stakes enterprise. The cost of television rights runs into the billions of dollars, and the enormous viewing audiences for the opening and closing ceremonies, which generate huge advertising revenue, are key to the financial viability of Olympic coverage. "Nothing focuses world attention more than the Olympic ceremonies," insists Don Mischer, veteran producer-director of the ceremonies, including those of the 1996 Centennial Games in Atlanta and the 2002 Salt Lake City Games. "You spend three years worrying about what you're doing and whether you're doing it right. Are we sending the right message? In Atlanta we had a cast of 8,000. We had over 3,000 volunteers. We had 400 on our staff. But the toughest thing by far is deciding what are you going to be putting down there on that field?"

The years of creative and logistical preparations for the opening ceremony all come down to the presentation of the final legs of the torch run, and key to the buildup is the mystery surrounding the identities of the final torchbearers. For the 1996 Summer Games, NBC Television had the

broadcast rights. Don Mischer recalls how the process of choosing the person to light the Olympic flame began: "Dick Ebersol [president of NBC Sports] and I were having dinner in Atlanta. It was the early part of April, and we were just spitballing names back and forth, and I think Dick brought Ali's name up. And it really seemed right for so many reasons. I mean, what he was dealing with in his life. What he had overcome as an athlete. How true he was to his beliefs in a period of great turmoil in American history."

The next step was to present their idea to Billy Paine, head of the Atlanta Olympic Organizing Committee. "He

was hoping to get somebody who was born and raised in Georgia to light the flame," said Mischer. Paine asked for some time to mull it over; three weeks later he told Mischer and Ebersol to proceed with their choice. Now someone had to talk to Muhammad Ali.

To minimize the risk of revealing their idea, it was decided that Mischer and Paine would speak first to Howard Bingham, Ali's close confidant and personal photographer of many years. "Now, our offices were at Olympic Stadium in Atlanta," Mischer said. "And I knew that if Howard Bingham came walking in, people were

heavyweight boxer still known as Cassius Clay, he defeated Zbigniew Pietrzykowski to win the gold medal. The 1960 Rome Olympics was the launchpad for Ali's amazing career. Atlanta would be his triumphant return.

Ten days before the opening ceremony, Ali stealthily came to Atlanta for a rehearsal. Again, Mischer insisted on complete secrecy. "We knew that if we brought him anywhere near the stadium, word would get out. So we did it at three o'clock in the morning." Security guards were released, lights were turned off, and everybody was told to leave. Then Ali arrived alone in an unmarked car. "We used flashlights to bring him up the stairs to this little pathway where the flame would be run to him. We said, 'Janet Evans

The 1960 Rome Olympics was the launchpad for Ali's amazing career. Atlanta would be his triumphant return.

going to put two and two together and assume that we were talking to Ali. So we arranged to meet in a garbage room." The stacks of garbage were pushed aside to make room for a card table and three folding chairs, and Mischer, Paine, and Bingham met for an hour and a half.

Bingham agreed to relay their proposal to Ali, who was honored by the invitation. Thirty-six years had passed since Ali's first Olympic appearance in Rome. There, as a light

will come up right here. She'll hold up her torch to light yours. You'll take a moment, feel it. Then turn and light the device on the wire that will carry the flame to the top.'

"Well he wasn't talking much," observed Mischer. "He was just watching. And then I said, 'Champ, do you feel okay about this? I mean, is this something that you want to do? You deserve to do it. And we hope you will. But do you feel okay about it?' And he doubled up his fist and gave me a pretend jab in the stomach"—Mischer laughs—"and then broke into a big smile."

The opening ceremony for the 1996 Centennial Olympic Games took place on July 19. The torch run, which began 84 days earlier, on April 27 in Los Angeles, had covered 15,000 miles. Bob Costas and Dick Enberg hosted the event for NBC.

Once the ceremony was under way, Ali was taken to a heavily guarded holding room under the northeast corner of the stadium. Then, as the ceremony was building to its climax, the large television screens inside the stadium showed legendary four-time gold medalist Al Oerter carrying the torch into the bowels of the stadium. Oerter handed it to a hometown hero, 1984 Olympian and former heavyweight champion Evander Holyfield. Holyfield sprinted around the track with Greek athlete Voula Patoulidou before handing the torch to American swimming champion Janet Evans. Evans, who had won three gold medals eight years earlier in Seoul, Korea, won gold and silver medals at the '92 Barcelona Games, and was back for one last set of competitive laps in the Olympic pool at Atlanta, began her ascent to the platform where the lighting ceremony would take place.

As Evans climbed to the strains of Beethoven's "Ode to Joy," the crowd seemed to be breaking decibel levels; the anticipation was palpable. When she neared the top of the platform, Ali stepped out from the shadows. Costas—whose voice revealed both surprise and approval—said simply, "But look who gets it next."

"The Greatest," Enberg remarked excitedly, before adding his signature "Oh my!" And one Olympic champion handed the torch to another.

Left to right: Evander Holyfield and Greek athlete Voula Patoulidou carry the torch around the stadium track, passing it to swimming champion Janet Evans. ■ At the top of the platform, Evans passed the flame to Ali. ■ Ali stands alone with the torch aloft.

As Ali stood alone on the platform, the cheering reverberated in a cacophony of appreciation. Despite the visible effects of Ali's Parkinson's disease, Costas underscored his presence as "still exuding nobility and stature" and said,

"The response he evokes is part affection, part excitement, but especially respect. What a moment."

"I remember getting goose bumps. I got tears in my eyes," recalls Mischer, who was directing the world television feed from the control room beneath Olympic Stadium. "You work for years hoping that you get that kind of response out of an audience. And it just felt very gratifying."

As soon as the cauldron was lit, Ali was led away and driven into the night. He had electrified the Games. The man who at one time fought to hear people call him by the name he had chosen, on that night—as he added perhaps the final brick to his own legendary Olympian edifice—heard the crowd roaring: "Ali. Ali. Ali."

"And he doubled up his fist and gave me a pretend jab in the stomach . . . and then broke into a big smile."

Left to right: The champ uses the torch to light the Olympic flame. ▪ The Olympic flame burns in the cauldron above the illuminated scaffolding.

Tiger's Win for the Ages

Left to right: Putting on the third green. ■ *Tense crowds watched Woods's every move, as did millions of television viewers around the world.*

April 13, 1997

H e said before he even entered college that his goal was to win more major championships than any golfer in history, including Nicklaus," said CBS sportscaster Jim Nantz to the unprecedented viewing audience tuned in to watch 21-year-old Tiger Woods play in his first Masters Tournament.

The Masters, one of golf's oldest and most prestigious tournaments, dates back to 1934 and is played each year at the Augusta National Golf Club, an exclusive course nestled in the lush rolling hills outside Augusta, Georgia, designed by golfing legend Bobby Jones. But like many southern institutions, Augusta National and its tournament were slow to integrate; it wasn't until 1975 that a black player was allowed to compete in the tournament, and Augusta National's own membership did not include a black member until the early 1990s. "So he'll chase Jack Nicklaus," Nantz continued, "but he follows Jackie Robinson as a man who broke barriers—men who transcended their sport."

As Woods began his pursuit of the coveted green jacket, his opening drive on the opening tee of the opening day of the 1997 Masters was an uncharacteristically errant shot—

hardly what might be expected from golf's former child prodigy. This was the kid who started swinging a golf club when his peers were still playing on swings, the kid who was on television putting against Bob Hope at the age of two, the kid who shot a 48 for nine holes at the age of three, the kid who was the subject of a feature story in *Golf Digest* at the age of five.

After a brilliant amateur career, which included the 1996 NCAA championship as an undergraduate at Stanford University, Woods turned pro in 1996. He had already won three of the 14 pro tournaments he had entered by the time he arrived at the Augusta National Golf Club at age 21. But to live up to the hoopla surrounding his entry, Woods would not only have to play well, he would have to win the Masters.

Instead, he turned out to be human and perhaps a little shaken by the high expectations. After that first bad shot, he put his hand over his mouth and stared down the fairway, seemingly in disbelief that such a drive could have come from his hands. Finally, Woods shook his head in disgust and moved on. He bogeyed the first hole, and the fourth and the eighth and the ninth. Woods shot a 40 for the first nine holes. The highest score ever for the front nine on opening day for an eventual Masters winner had been a 38.

But then he steadied himself. The steely gaze was back. The sure, powerful stroke was operating. The deadly

Left to right: Woods is jubilant on the 18th green after making the winning putt. ■ Mobbed by the press, he embraces his father and then tries on the famous green jacket.

show that April the 11th, 1997, at 5:42, Tiger Woods has taken the lead at the Masters for the first time in his career."

Woods had found his rhythm and wouldn't lose it again that memorable weekend as he soared into golf's elite circle of legends. He followed his opening round of 70 with a 66 and a 65. At one point, he went 37 holes without a bogey.

Woods entered the final round an incredible 15 under par with a nine-stroke lead over runner-up Constantino Rocca. And now the praise and the awe were coming not only from the media and the fans, but from Woods's hardened contemporaries. Tom Watson said Woods might be the type of player who comes around only once in a millennium. Ben Crenshaw said he couldn't find the words to describe Woods's performance. "When I first heard about him," Tom Kite told the *Los Angeles Times*, "he was about eight. I don't get scared of eight-year-olds. But they do grow up."

The old master himself, Jack Nicklaus, winner of six Masters, conceded his throne to this young phenom. "It's a shame [Bobby] Jones isn't here," Nicklaus said. "He could have saved the words he used for me in 1963 for this young man, because he is certainly playing a game we're not familiar with."

The night before the final round, Woods's father, Earl, who nicknamed his son after a soldier he knew in Vietnam and was the first to put a club in young Tiger's hands, had a talk with his son. "He said," Tiger recalled, "'Son, this will be probably one of the hardest rounds you have ever had to play in your life. If you just go out there and be yourself, it will be one of the most rewarding rounds of golf you have ever played in your life.' And he was right."

By the time Woods took the historic march up the 18th fairway, he was no longer merely a competitor in a tournament. He was at a golfing coronation—his own.

His father, who was prevented from walking the final round by a heart ailment, was waiting at the 18th green after watching his son blaze through hole after hole on a television monitor. "The dream," said the senior Woods, "has now turned into reality."

At the end, victory long assured, Woods still needed to make a four-foot putt on the last hole to break the Masters'

putting eye was focused. On the back nine, Woods got four birdies, and an eagle on the par-five 15th hole. The Tiger Woods everybody had come to see had shown up after all. He took an astonishing ten strokes off on the back nine, shooting a 30.

During Friday's round, any remnant of doubt about Woods was eliminated when he took the lead for the first time after sinking an eagle putt on the 13th green, a moment so significant in golfing history that Jim Nantz felt compelled to memorialize it in the broadcast. "Let the record all-time scoring record of 270, held jointly by Nicklaus (1965) and Raymond Floyd (1976). The packed gallery at the 18th hole was hushed as they watched Woods study the terrain of the green. In a whispered tone, CBS commentator Jim Nantz underscored the historic Masters moment. "The depth of this kid's preparation for this stage at this moment just runs so deep," he said. "There's no doubt in my mind that he's very aware of the significance of this putt in terms of the tournament scoring record."

Playing the slight break, Woods drew back his putter and tapped the ball with precision. As the ball hit the bottom of the cup the gallery erupted. "A win for the ages!" shouted Nantz. Tiger pumped the air twice with his fist in elation, and threw his arms around his father for a long embrace that drew out all the pent-up emotion of Woods's wondrous four days at Augusta, an image no one who watched will ever for-

"Tiger Woods . . . shattering record, after record, after record."

get. "Tiger Woods, in a moment like no one has ever seen at the Masters," said Nantz, "shattering record, after record, after record."

The fortunes of golf and television changed dramatically following the Masters in 1997. An estimated 43 million people tuned in to watch Woods's triumph, the largest view-

ing audience to date for the Masters. Woods was responsible for golf being viewed in households where it had not appeared before. According to CBS Sports president Sean McManus, "When it comes to Tiger Woods and the Masters, people have a keen interest in wanting to witness history."

Woods had lived up to his promise in spectacular fashion, breaking one standard after another in golf's premier event. Woods was 18 under par, the lowest in any major tournament in the 20th century, and won by 12 strokes, three more than the greatest previous Masters margin. He was the youngest to win the Masters by two years, having surpassed Seve Ballesteros, who had set the record at 23, and was only the second golfer to win the first major event he entered, the other being Jerry Pate, who debuted with a victory in the 1976 U.S. Open. Being of both African American and Asian American descent, Woods was the first of either race to win a golf major.

It would be four more years before Woods won another Masters. But he was victorious in both 2001 and 2002, putting him, at age 26, halfway to Nicklaus's feat of winning the event six times—and on course to fulfill the prediction of those who say Woods will ultimately be the master of them all.

Acknowledgments

I t would be nearly impossible to bring a book like this to fruition if it were not for the inexhaustible contributions of many talented and dedicated people. I'm blessed to be surrounded by so many.

My sincerest gratitude to Kathleen Andrews, John McMeel, Tom Thornton, and Hugh Andrews for believing in and committing to this endeavor. A special thank-you to my agent, Sloan Harris, for bringing us together.

I am extremely grateful to Chris Schillig for her steadfast guidance, patience, and enthusiasm throughout.

My heartfelt thank-you to Maura Kelley. Her contributions to this book are immeasurable. She met each challenge—and there were many—with enthusiasm and determination, and I am grateful.

Words seem insufficient to express my gratitude to Bob Costas, Walter Cronkite, and Dick Van Dyke. Each exemplifies the very best in their television genre, and to have them hosting the television moments is the highest honor and compliment this book could be paid.

I would also like to thank Pam Davis, business manager and assistant to Bob Costas; Marlene Adler, chief of staff to Walter Cronkite; and Brooke Slavik of the William Morris Agency, for skillfully facilitating the seemingly endless details associated with the production.

I am grateful to designer Holly Camerlinck, copy chief Michelle Daniel, and administrative assistant JuJu Johnson of Andrews McMeel Publishing for applying their considerable talents and energy to helping me with production of the book.

Thank you to Chris Monte and Jim Castle for their tireless commitment and generous contributions of their talent, creativity, and experience, and to Kris Wilson for graciously sharing his expertise at times when it was truly needed.

Thank you to Louise Argianas of ABC Sports and Deanna O'Toole at CBS Sports for their continued enthusiasm, encouragement, and support, and to Jeff Sotzing at Carson Productions, who always greeted my numerous questions and requests in such a helpful and friendly manner. Thank you to Jill and Hilary Cosell for graciously allowing me to include moments made unforgettable by their father, the legendary Howard Cosell.

I would like to extend my sincerest gratitude to Wendy Heller-Stein for her loyalty and willingness to share her invaluable knowledge.

Thank you to Andy Darrow and Andy Velcoff for their friendship and their guidance, helping to open doors and cut through red tape.

Thank you to Gregg Oppenheimer, author of *Laughs, Luck . . . and Lucy* (lucynet.com), for his generous contribution of *I Love Lucy* photos.

I am particularly grateful to Lorra-Lea Bartlett at CBS Entertainment, Ruth Engelhardt at Calvada Productions, Edward Zimmerman at Columbia TriStar Domestic Television, Valerie C. Bruce at Broadway Video Enterprises, Marlene Eastman at Warner Bros. Television, Andy Bandit at 20th Century Fox Television, Charlie Parsons at Castaway Television Productions Ltd., Andrew Solt and Beatrice McMillan at SOFA Entertainment, Gary Hovey at Elvis Presley Enterprises, Inc., Max Segal at HBO, Brian Fulford at CNN Image Source, Chris Miller at ABC News VideoSource, Tony Bracket at ABC News, Yuien Chin and Barbara Kramer at NBC News Archive, Toni Gavin and Patricia Vanderbeek at CBS News Archive, Dina Panto at Major League Baseball Properties, Nancy Behar at the NFL, Linda Sponaugle at NFL Films, Donna Johnson at Augusta National Golf Club, Alan Goodrich at the John F. Kennedy Library and Museum, and Michael Goodell at BBC Worldwide for seeing the vision and clearing the way to enable us to include these unforgettable television moments.

Thank you to the following people for their determination in providing us with the very best images: Jim Lee at AllSport, Jodi Helman at *Sports Illustrated*, Rosa DiSalvo at Archive Photo, Henry McGee at Globe Photo, Inc., David Lombard at CBS Photo Archive, Elisabeth Edwards at Desilu, too, Ann Limongello at ABC Photo Archive, Susan Naulty at the Richard Nixon Library and Birthplace, Steve Branch and Jason Tenenbaum at the Ronald Reagan Presidential Library, Kelly Hill at Elvis Presley Enterprises, Rita Wilson at the Lyndon Baines Johnson Library, Jonathan Hyams at Michael Ochs Archive, and Scott Macrillo at NFL Photos. And a special thank-you to Wendy Rysanek and Jeffrey Dreyfuss at Corbis Images, and Jeni Rosenthal at AP Wide World, for going above and beyond.

Thank you to Janel Syverud for keeping the business running while I was running in all directions.

Thank you to Dixon Smith and Mark Biase at the Production Group, Sharon DiTullio at National Video Center, Tom Gibis at Dick Clark Productions, and Caetera Collins at the Belage Hotel Los Angeles.

A special thank-you to Dan and Kelly Bennett, Vito and Gabriela Costanzo, Wayne and Monica Tweddell, John and Sharman Borncamp, and James and Jeanette VanMeter for their friendship and for being surrogate families to mine during the longest days of this project, and to Jennifer Borncamp specifically for inspiring my choice of hosts. A special thank-you as well to Jerry and Sandi Barnes for their love and support.

And as always, to my parents, Jim and Betty Garner, for their endless love and encouragement, and for allowing me to watch TV.

Credits

Authored and produced by Joe Garner.

Editorial/text assistance provided by David Davis, Paul Feinberg, Stuart Miller, Steve Springer, and Bill Stroum.

Narration written by Mark Rowland.

Interview assistance provided by Barry Freeman and Evan Haning.

Research provided by Michael Dolan.

DVD chapters coproduced and edited by Chris Monte, Magic Hair, Inc.
Additional editing provided by Jason Cherella and Justin Hixon.
DVD graphics and menu designed by Jim Castle, Castle Digital Design, Inc.
DVD coordinating producer Maura Kelley.
Audio production engineering by Mike Forslund. Engineering production assistant Nancy Forslund.

Camera and sound for interviews provided by Jason Miller and Alex Van Wagner.

Video clips provided by and copyright of:

ABC News

ABC Sports, Inc.

ABC Video Source

Augusta National Golf Club

BBC Television

Broadway Video Enterprises and NBC Studios

Calvada Productions

Carson Productions

Castaway Television Productions

CBS Entertainment, Inc.

CBS News Archive

CBS Sports, Inc.

CNN
Columbia TriStar Domestic Television
Desilu, too
HBO Sports
Major League Baseball Properties, Inc.
NBC News Archive

NBC Sports, Inc.
NFL Footage © NFL Productions LLC 2002
Paramount Television
U.S. Olympic Committee
Warner Bros. Television

The Ed Sullivan Show courtesy of SOFA Entertainment.

Footage from "*M*A*S*H*—Goodbye Farewell" courtesy of 20th Century Fox Television. All rights reserved.

"The Fund Crisis Speech" provided with permission of the Republican National Committee and the Richard Nixon Library and Birthplace.

Portions of footage of O. J. Simpson pursuit provided courtesy of the Los Angeles News Service.

Portions of footage of the rescue of Jessica McClure provided by KWES TV, Midland, Texas.

The Nixon-Gannon interviews provided courtesy of the University of Georgia Libraries Media Archives and Peabody Awards Collection.

"Ready Teddy"
Words and music by Robert Blackwell and John S. Marascalco.
© 1956, 1984 Elvis Presley Music
All rights administered by Chrysalis Songs (BMI).
Copyright renewed. International copyright secured.
All rights reserved. Used by permission.
"Ready Teddy"
Words and music by John Marascalco and Robert Blackwell.
Copyright © 1956 Elvis Presley Music (BMI)/Venice Music Corp. (BMI).
Worldwide Rights for Elvis Presley Music and Venice Music Corp.
administered by Cherry River Music Co. (BMI) and Chrysalis Standards, Inc. (BMI).
All Rights Reserved   Used By Permission

The name, image, and likeness of Elvis Presley appears courtesy of Elvis Presley Enterprises, Inc.

A very special thank-you to the following people for their generosity of time and insight: Aaron Brown, Joe Buck, Mark Burnett, Bob Carroll Jr., Dick Cline, Mary Crosby, Loraine Despres, George Eckstein, D. J. Fontana, Frank Gifford, Don Hewitt, Norman Lear, Dennis Lewin, Maureen McCormick, Ed McMahon, Burt Metcalfe, Al Michaels, Lorne Michaels, Don Mischer, Scotty Moore, Jim Nantz, Jeff Probst, Madelyn Pugh-Davis, John Ratzenberger, Carl Reiner, Cathy Rigby, Tim Russert, Lloyd Schwartz, Tommie Smith, Sally Struthers, and Robert and Marika Tur.

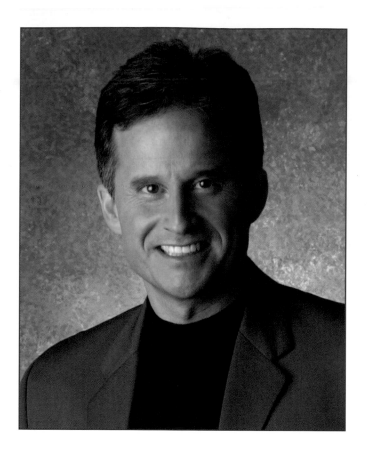

Joe Garner | Proclaimed by pre-

eminent talk-show host Larry King as "the Ken Burns of the written and taped word," author-producer Joe Garner is a pioneer in multimedia publishing. Garner's passion for broadcast history and documentary-style publishing has resulted in three *New York Times* best-sellers, *We Interrupt This Broadcast*, *And the Crowd Goes Wild*, and *And the Fans Roared*, making him the most successful multimedia author in publishing. Garner is a frequent guest on talk radio and has appeared on many national television talk shows, including *Larry King Live*, Fox News Channel's *Fox & Friends*, NBC's *Weekend Today*, and *The Late Late Show with Craig Kilborn*. Garner's books have also appeared on best-seller lists in *Publishers Weekly*, the *Wall Street Journal*, and *USA Today*.

Bob Costas | Bob Costas has been with NBC Sports since 1979. During that time, he

has covered every major sport but is perhaps most identified with the Olympics and baseball. He anchored NBC's prime-time coverage of the last three Summer Olympics—Barcelona 1992, Atlanta 1996, and Sydney, Australia, in 2000—as well as the Winter Games in Salt Lake City in 2002. From 1983 through 1989, Costas teamed with Tony Kubek on NBC's baseball *Game of the Week* telecasts, and he hosted the network's *NFL Live* pregame show from 1984 to 1992. Costas has been involved in the coverage of six league championship series and five World Series for NBC Sports. He has hosted six Super Bowls and served as the play-by-play voice of the NBA on NBC from 1997 to 2000. In February 2001, HBO launched *"On the Record" with Bob Costas*, a weekly hour-long program of issues, interviews, and commentary.

Costas has won 13 Emmy Awards—nine as outstanding sports broadcaster, two for writing, one for his late-night interview show, *Later with Bob Costas*, and one for his play-by-play broadcast of the 1997 World Series. He has been named National Sportscaster of the Year by his peers an unprecedented seven times—in 1985, 1988, 1991, 1992, 1995, 1997, and 2000. When he first won the NSSA Award in 1985, he was 33 years old, the youngest announcer to be so honored.

Bob Costas is a frequent contributor to NBC News as a reporter and interviewer on the *Today* show and other network programs. He is also the author of the *New York Times* best-seller *Fair Ball: A Fan's Case for Baseball*.

Walter Cronkite

Walter Cronkite has covered virtually every major news event during his more than 60 years in journalism—the last 50 affiliated with CBS News. For nineteen years he was anchorman and managing editor of the *CBS Evening News*. His accomplishments—both on air and off—have won him acclaim and trust from journalism colleagues and the American public alike.

Following his departure from the *CBS Evening News* in 1981, Cronkite hosted several acclaimed CBS documentary programs, including the Emmy-winning *Children of Apartheid* and the CBS News science magazine series *Walter Cronkite's Universe*. In 1985, he was inducted into the Academy of Television Arts and Sciences Hall of Fame.

Walter Cronkite was the only journalist to be voted among the Top Ten Most Influential Decision Makers in America in surveys conducted by *U.S. News and World Report*; he was also named Most Influential Person in Broadcasting. In a nationwide viewer opinion survey conducted as recently as 1995, more than a decade after he left the CBS anchor desk, he was voted Most Trusted Man in Television News.

In addition to his ongoing assignments as a special correspondent for CBS, Cronkite maintains a demanding international lecture and public appearance schedule and hosts many public affairs and cultural programs. In 1993, he cofounded the Cronkite Ward Company, which has produced more than 60 hours of award-winning documentaries for the Discovery Channel, PBS, and other networks. In 1996, Cronkite's production company, in collaboration with CBS and the Discovery Channel, produced his memoirs, entitled *Cronkite Remembers*. The two-hour CBS special aired in May of that year, and the eight-hour series premiered later on the Discovery Channel. Also in 1996, Cronkite published his best-selling autobiography, *A Reporter's Life*.

Dick Van Dyke

During his 50-plus years in show business, Dick Van Dyke has starred in Broadway hits, classic movies, and matchless television shows, taking home five Emmy Awards and a Tony. Recent years have brought new honors: the Dance Legend of the Year Award from the Professional Dancers Society of America (1999), the 1998 Disney Legend Award, induction into the Academy of Television Arts and Sciences Hall of Fame (1995), a Lifetime Achievement Award from the American Comedy Awards, and a star on the Hollywood Walk of Fame (1993). Earlier, his classic television comedy series *The Dick Van Dyke Show*, which is still in syndication 40 years after its premiere, was placed in the Producers Guild Hall of Fame.

After winning his Tony for his performance in the smash hit *Bye Bye Birdie* (1961), Van Dyke subsequently appeared in the 1979 revival of *The Music Man* and toured in *Damn Yankees*. His movie credits include *Bye Bye Birdie* (1963), *What a Way to Go* (1964), *Mary Poppins* (1964), *Divorce American Style* (1967), *Chitty Chitty Bang Bang* (1968), *The Comic* (1969), *Some Kind of a Nut* (1969), *Cold Turkey* (1971), and *The Runner Stumbles* (1979).

In February 2002, Dick Van Dyke starred in the CBS television movie *Town Without Pity*, playing the smarter-than-he-acts Dr. Mark Sloane, his character for nine seasons in *Diagnosis Murder*, now in worldwide syndication.

Photography Credits

All photos included in the *Stay Tuned* book are listed by page number, in left to right order.

4 Corbis, CBS Photo Archive; 5 Corbis, Desilu, too, LLC; 6 CBS Photo Archive; 7 CBS Entertainment, All CBS Photo Archive; 8 CBS Photo Archive, Corbis; 9 Corbis, CBS Photo Archive; 10 All CBS Photo Archive; 11 Corbis, Corbis, CBS Photo Archive; 12 Calvada Productions; 13 CBS Photo Archive, Michael Ochs Archives, Michael Ochs Archives; 14 All CBS Photo Archive; 15 Calvada Productions, Corbis; 16 Associated Press/HO, ©ABC Photography Archives; 17 All Corbis; 18 All © ABC Photography Archive; 19 ©ABC Photography Archive, Michael Ochs Archives, © ABC Photography Archive; 20 Michael Ochs Archives, CBS Photo Archive; 21 Michael Ochs Archives, Corbis, BMI/Michael Ochs Archives; 22 All Corbis; 23 All CBS Photo Archive; 24 All Michael Ochs Archives; 25 All Michael Ochs Archives; 26 Michael Ochs Archives; 27 All Michael Ochs Archives; 28 All Globe Photos, Inc.; 29 Corbis, NBC/Globe Photos, Inc.; 30 All Corbis; 31 Corbis; 32 NBC/Globe Photos, Inc.; 33 Corbis, Broadway Video Enterprises and NBC Studios; 34 All Michael Ochs Archives; 35 Michael Ochs Archives; 36 Corbis, Lorimar Productions; 37 Lorimar Productions; 38–43 All 20th Century Fox; 44 All NBC/Globe Photos, Inc.; 45 All NBC/Globe Photos, Inc.; 46–47 All NBC/Globe Photos, Inc.; 48 NBC/Globe Photos, Inc., Carroll Seghers II/Globe Photos; 49 NBC/Globe Photos, Inc., NBC Globe Photos, Inc., Globe Photos, Inc.; 50 Suzie Bleeden/Globe Photos, Inc., Carson Productions; 51 All NBC/Globe Photos, Inc.; 52 Suzie Bleeden/Globe Photos, Inc., Globe Photos, Inc., Globe Photos, Inc.; 53 Alice S. Hall/Globe Photos, Inc., Carson Productions; 54 All CBS Photo Archive; 55 CBS Photo Archive, CBS Entertainment, Inc.; 56 CBS Photo Archives, CBS Entertainment, Inc.; 57 All CBS Photo Archive; 60 Corbis, *New York Post*/Richard Nixon Library and Birthplace; 61 Richard Nixon Library and Birthplace; 62 All Corbis; 63 Richard Nixon Library and Birthplace, *Daily Mirror*/Richard Nixon Library and Birthplace; 64–67 All Corbis; 68 All AP Wide World Photos; 69 CBS Photo Archive; 70 Corbis; 71 Corbis, AP Wide World Photos/*Dallas Morning News*; 72 All Corbis; 73 Corbis, AP Wide World Photos; 74 Lyndon Baines Johnson's Presidential Library, Corbis; 75 All CBS Photo Archive; 76 CBS News Archive; 77 Lyndon Baines Johnson's Presidential Library; 78 AP Wide World Photos/NASA, Corbis, Corbis; 79 Corbis; 80 All AP Wide World Photos; 81 Corbis, AP Wide World Photos/NASA, AP/Wide World Photos; 82 Corbis, Corbis, AP Wide World Photos; 83 AP Wide World Photos, Corbis, Corbis, Corbis; 84 Corbis; 85 Richard Nixon Library and Birthplace, Corbis; 86 Corbis, Corbis, AP Wide World Photos; 87 All Corbis; 88 Corbis, Corbis, AP Wide World Photos; 89 Corbis, AP Wide World Photos; 90 All Corbis; 91 All AP Wide World Photos; 92 All AP Wide World Photos; 93 All Corbis; 94 Corbis, AP Wide World Photos/APTV; 95 All AP Wide World Photos/Reuters Pool; 96 Liaison, KWES-TV Midland, Texas; 97 Liaison; 98 Corbis, KWES-TV Midland, Texas; 99 Liaison, Corbis; 100 All AP Wide World Photos; 101 Corbis; 102 Corbis; 103 Corbis, Ronald Reagan Library, AP Wide World Photos; 104 Corbis, AP Wide World Photos; 105 AP Wide World Photos, AP Wide World Photos/*The Leavenworth Times*, Corbis; 106–107 All Corbis; 108 AP Wide World Photos, Corbis; 109 AP Wide World Photos, Corbis; 110 AP Wide World Photos; 111 All Corbis; 112–115 All Corbis; 116 Corbis, CNN, Corbis; 117 AP Wide World Photos, Corbis; 118 AP Wide World Photos, AP Wide World Photos/KHBS, KHOG; 119 CNN, Corbis; 120 AP Wide World Photos, Getty Images; 121 Corbis, AP Wide World Photos, Corbis; 122 AP Wide World Photos, Corbis, Corbis; 123 Corbis, © 2001 *The Record* (Bergen County, NJ), Thomas E. Franklin, Staff Photographer/Corbis; 126 All © ABC Photography Archive; 127 © ABC Photography Archive, *Sports Illustrated*, © ABC Photography Archive; 128 © ABC Photography Archive, AP/Wide World Photos; 129 Corbis, © ABC Photography Archive; 130 AP Wide World Photos; 131 Corbis, AP Wide World Photos, Corbis; 132 All Allsport; 133 Allsport, Allsport, AP Wide World Photos; 134 AP Wide World Photos, Harry How/Getty Images; 135 All Corbis; 136 Archive Photo/Popperfoto; 137 Corbis, Corbis, *Sports Illustrated*/James Drake; 138 *Sports Illustrated*/Neil Leifer; 139 Corbis, *Sports Illustrated*/Rich Clarkson; 140 © Malcolm Emmons/NFL Photos, Globe Photos, Inc./Russ Reed; 141 Corbis, AP Wide World Photos; 142 Corbis, Corbis, Globe Photos, Inc./Russ Reed; 143 All © Russ Reed/NFL Photos; 144 © ABC Photography Archive, AP Wide World Photos, © ABC Photography Archive; 145–147 All © ABC Photography Archive; 148 AP Wide World Photos, © ABC Photography Archive; 149 © ABC Photography Archive, © ABC Photography Archive, Corbis; 150 AP Wide World Photos, Corbis; 151 Corbis, © ABC Photography Archive, © ABC Photography Archive; 152 Corbis; 153 Corbis, AP Wide World Photos, Corbis; 154–155 All Corbis; 156 Heinz Kluetmeier/*Sports Illustrated*, *Sports Illustrated*/Walter Iooss Jr., Allsport/Don Morley; 157 Hulton Deutsch/Allsport, AP Wide World Photos; 158 © ABC Photography Archive, *Sports Illustrated*; 159 All © ABC Photography Archive; 160 All AP Wide World Photos; 161 Corbis, © ABC Photography Archive; 162 AP Wide World Photos, © ABC Photography Archive; 163 Corbis; 164 AP Wide World Photos; 165 All *Sports Illustrated*/Heinz Kluetmeier; 166 All AP Wide World Photos; 167 Corbis; 168 Corbis, AP Wide World Photos; 169 Allsport; 170 AP Wide World Photos; 171 Corbis; 172 All AP Wide Word Photos; 173 Corbis, *Sports Illustrated*; 174 Corbis; 175 AP Wide World Photo, *Sports Illustrated*.

Additional photos included on the *Stay Tuned* DVD were provided by 20th Century Fox Television, © ABC Photography Archive, AP Wide World Photos, CBS Photo Archive, Corbis, Getty Images, Lyndon Baines Johnson's Presidential Library, Michael Ochs Archives, NBC/Globe Photos, Inc., NFL Photos, Richard Nixon Library and Birthplace, *Sports Illustrated*.